281

CONFIDENT CHILDREN

CONFIDENT CHILDREN

Developing Your Child's Self-esteem

Glen Stenhouse

Illustrations by Jennifer Lautusi

Auckland
OXFORD UNIVERSITY PRESS
Melbourne   Oxford   New York

Oxford University Press, Walton Street, Oxford OX2 6DP
Oxford   New York   Toronto
Delhi   Bombay   Calcutta   Madras   Karachi
Kuala Lumpur   Singapore   Hong Kong   Tokyo
Nairobi   Dar es Salaam   Cape Town
Melbourne   Auckland   Madrid
and associated companies in
Berlin   Ibadan

Oxford is a trade mark of Oxford University Press

This edition first published 1994

ISBN   0 19 558314 0

Cover designed by Jacinda Torrance/Paradigm
Set in Palatino by Scope
Printed in Australia
Published by Oxford University Press
1A Matai Road, Greenlane
PO Box 11-149, Auckland, New Zealand

Contents

1

Self-esteem

We have the power as parents to give our children a priceless legacy: a sense of self-esteem. It is not a gift we give through inheritance, because self-esteem does not come with our genes. It is created by our experiences and begins to be shaped from the earliest years of our life. As parents, we play a major role in that process of shaping.

This book is written to guide parents who want to help their children to grow up with a positive self-concept, a sense of self-worth, a feeling that they are OK as people. We will look at dimensions of parenting, such as love, respect, listening, praise, the use of power, and encouraging independence, all of which have an influence on how self-esteem develops. We will also discuss the powerful effect that school can have on a child's self-concept, the issues of identity and gender, and what can be done for children whose self-worth has been damaged.

Whatever talents, strengths, and potential a child is born with may come to nothing unless activated and given direction by a sense of self-esteem. Low self-esteem can not only sap a child's natural optimism and zest for living, but, in the worst case, can convert these positive forces into a harmful energy directed at both self and society. This book will, I hope, show you how to make the development of your child's self-esteem a natural focus and theme in your parenting.

In this book I have drawn on twenty years' experience as a child psychologist, educator, and parent. Much of what I say may already be familiar to you, but I have tried to present accepted facts and even mundane truths about good parenting in the light of their effect on self-esteem. Because of this I hope you will gain some new perspectives on what you may already know and be doing, as well as fresh insights into how you can help your child to grow and fulfil her or his potential with confidence.

This book is clearly not an encyclopaedia covering every aspect of the subject, or every possible factor that might affect the development of a child's self-esteem, but there is more than enough in it for practical purposes. I can assure you that if you are trying to put most of its major recommendations into practice (and I stress the word 'trying'), then self-esteem is one problem you shouldn't have to worry about with your child.

Self-esteem and Confidence

Our confidence in facing up to and coping with the many challenges we experience in life, and our personal adjustment as effective, independent, and emotionally stable adults, is associated with having a positive self-concept. The reverse, of course, is also true: lack of confidence and less adequate personal adjustment are associated with a negative self-concept. The relationship between good personal adjustment and self-esteem works both ways. A positive self-concept enables us to approach challenges confidently and therefore increases our chances of a successful outcome, and then each successful outcome enhances our self-esteem and boosts our confidence. The reverse relationship, between low self-esteem and less effective functioning as a person, is also true.

Extensive research over many years has shown that there is a clear relationship between a positive self-concept and successful functioning in a wide range of human activities, just as there is between a negative self-concept and some of the destructive behaviours that cause major problems in our society. So, if we do all we can to encourage the development of high self-esteem in our children, we are giving them the best possible opportunity to fulfil their potential both as unique individuals and as productive members of society. We are, in fact, giving them a head start in life.

What is the Self-concept?

We are probably the only species on the planet that has a sense of self, or an awareness of ourselves as individuals. At a common sense level, it seems easy to understand the 'self' as an aspect of our lives but it is in fact an elusive idea defying accurate definition. To capture its meaning and essence involves the discussion of complex psychological issues that go to the very heart of what it means to be human, and such a discussion is a little beyond the scope of this book! So we will make do with simpler, everyday, working definitions of some of the terms we will be using frequently. The first one is 'self-concept'.

Our self-concept is a kind of jigsaw puzzle put together from all those physical, psychological, and behavioural characteristics that make us the individuals we are. Each piece in the puzzle is a different aspect of ourselves, such as our gender, the things we like to do, what we're good at, the things that make us anxious, our history of happy or unhappy experiences, of success and failure, our perception of how we perform in different situations, our ideals, and our physical appearance. In fact, almost all our experiences, behaviours, and personal characteristics have the potential to affect the image we create of ourselves. This overall image of what we are like as an individual is our self-concept.

Not only is our self-concept a complex, multi-faceted

picture, but we also tend to evaluate each of its individual components. That is, we can have either positive or negative feelings about the way we look, how we get on with others, our performance at work or school, whether we are living up to our goals, and so on. Most of us tend to judge ourselves continually against standards of how we would like to be, or feel that we should be. You might be able to imagine each of the pieces of the self-concept jigsaw puzzle as having a plus or minus sign on it according to how we evaluate that particular aspect of ourselves. If the sum of all these positive and negative signs is definitely on the credit side, our overall self-concept is likely to be positive. If the balance tips more towards the negative, so will our self-concept.

Self-esteem

Self-esteem is another way of referring to a positive or negative self-concept. If we feel generally OK about ourselves, and can give ourselves a good overall passing grade as a person, then we can say that we have a positive self-concept, a good self-image, or high self-esteem. Yet another option is to say that we have a sense of self-worth. If we give ourselves an overall failing grade as a person, then we would use such terms as negative self-concept, a poor or negative self-image, low self-esteem, or lack of self-worth.

We all have aspects of ourselves which we would like to be otherwise. If they are not too important we can live with them, and they don't upset us too much. But if we think that we are falling short in a significant aspect of our lives, it can have a powerful effect on how we feel about ourselves as people. That is, it can have a negative impact on our self-esteem.

Certain dimensions of life have a fundamental effect on how we see and evaluate ourselves, such as our physical appearance, how we relate to others, and whether we are successful in our work. If we feel uncomfortable about an aspect of our body image, unsuccessful in our social relationships, or stuck in a low-status, low-paid job (or the unemployment queue), it can negatively affect our overall self-image. That is because these dimensions of life are regarded as important in our society, and therefore carry greater weight in our evaluation of ourselves. They affect our self-esteem, and this in turn affects our basic approach to life, making it either positive and confident, or hesitant, pessimistic, and self-defeating.

For each of us there may also be areas of our life which are very important to us as individuals, such as a particular talent or skill (growing prize-winning roses), meeting certain behaviour standards (as in belonging to a church), or attaining certain personal goals (lowering a golf handicap). Because these aspects of our life are important to us, though perhaps not to society at large, they also can have a significant association with our overall self-concept, and so with our self-esteem. You will no doubt be able to think of one or two things that are an important part of your self-image, or that gave a real boost to your self-esteem when you achieved them, which others might not consider of much account.

For children, there are a few major issues that will have a powerful impact on their self-esteem. First and most important is whether they feel loved and valued by their parents. This, as we will discuss in the next chapter, is the foundation of a child's sense of security and self-worth, and influences self-esteem throughout childhood . As the child grows, the following factors become increasingly potent: success in school, the ability to make and keep friends, and, in the teenage years, physical appearance. Because of their importance, these factors have the power to influence a child's overall self-concept and sense of self-esteem.

What may seem like small victories or failures from

our adult perspective have the potential for major impact on children's self-concept and confidence, particularly in an area where they compare their own performance with that of their peers. A good example with young boys is learning physical skills, such as riding a bike, swimming, and ball games. Doing these things well means fame; being below par can mean sad times of being left out and the pain of a dented self-concept.

Relax!

It is definitely not the purpose of this book to make parents feel guilty about their parenting. The advice in these pages is meant to guide and support you in helping your child to develop a strong, positive self-concept, not to jab your conscience. Being a parent is a difficult job, and there will always be times when, because you are feeling tired, impatient, or generally dumped-on, you behave towards your child in ways that you regret almost immediately. That's OK. That's human. So long as our parenting is basically motivated by loving concern for our children, and so long as they know that we love them, there is actually a wide margin of error in being a successful parent. Children are amazingly resilient and forgiving. Occasional grumpiness, selfishness, and insensitivity on our part will do them no permanent damage.

If you are taking the trouble to read this book, that in itself says something positive about how you approach your responsibilities as a parent, and you may already be putting into practice much of what I suggest. Use these pages as an opportunity to reflect on what you are currently doing, pat yourself on the back for what is going well, and set some attainable goals in areas where you think change might be helpful. Then relax, and remember that there is no such creature as the perfect parent!

2

Love

For children to develop a sense of self-esteem, they need to feel that they are loved. Self-esteem is based on love in the same way that a house is built on a foundation. An unstable foundation means a shaky house, and we are unlikely to develop a secure sense of self-worth unless as children we have been loved unconditionally — no strings attached.

A Basic Human Need

Apart from the most basic biological drive for self-preservation — for food, shelter, and safety — our most important need as humans is to feel that another person cares for us. Love is essential for human psychological health. If we don't grow up feeling that we are loved and wanted, it is much more difficult for us to develop to our full potential as individuals and as contributing members of society. Children who do not experience the security of a loving relationship with their parents may develop an attitude to life of anxious self-doubt rather than one of basic trust in their own abilities and worth.

Fortunately for us all, little babies are usually very easy to love. No doubt as the result of evolution, babies elicit a loving and protective response from the adults who care for them. It is likely that characteristics such as a baby's facial features, its size, and perhaps even the kind of movements the baby makes, draw an automatic feeling of protective, caring concern from adults. Certainly a baby's cry is very difficult to ignore — it demands a response from us!

The same is true of toddlers and young children. Their physical appearance, and many of the things they do and say, are very appealing to us as adults, drawing us to them with a desire to interact with and care for them. One word to describe all the appealing characteristics that little children have is cuteness, which we experience as a feeling of wanting to look at, touch, and hold them. This can be felt not only by the child's parents but even by strangers, which is an indication of the strength of the 'signals' transmitted by the youngster, signals that say, 'Look after me!'

Developing a Bond

Parents usually develop a warm and intense bond with their baby, which goes far beyond a simple response to the child's physical appeal, and is demonstrated by caring for the baby's needs, holding and caressing it, talking to it, and sometimes simply gazing upon it with love.

This outpouring of love and caring from parent to child is intensified once the baby is able to respond in some way to the parents' attentions. The first smile is a very good example of this. I remember one first-time father telling me that, after their new-born baby boy had caused several weeks of little sleep for the parents and total disruption of their lives, he had been ready to take the baby back to the maternity hospital — until the baby smiled! All was forgiven! That magical moment when baby looked at dad and smiled meant that dad had finally emerged from the general background blur as a distinct object, and the smile can only mean that baby liked what he saw! This beginning of reciprocal responding — parent responds to baby who then responds

The baby looks at dad and smiles.

to parent, and so on — means that an increasingly stronger bond will be forged between parent and child.

Love Is Essential for Growth

So important is responsiveness from the parent, that without it a baby may retreat into withdrawal, unhappiness, and listlessness. This has been shown very clearly by studies of orphaned babies brought up in large institutions with minimal care other than for their basic physical needs, and lacking a consistent caregiver with whom to build a mutual relationship. Not only did these children become apathetic and emotionally withdrawn, but they also failed to show normal physical development, a condition known as 'failure to thrive'. Although this is obviously an extreme case of the effect of lack of love on children, there can be no clearer demonstration of how essential parental love is to a child's development. Just as plants need the sun to grow, so children need love.

How Do We Show Our Love?

How can we best express the love that we feel for our children? There are a number of obvious ways: by word, by gesture, and by caring for their needs. Exactly what we do will depend on our child's stage of development.

We express love for a baby in very direct and physical ways — by feeding, holding, comforting, caressing, talking to, and playing with it. We express love for toddlers by doing many of the same things, but with greater emphasis on talking to them, and by encouraging them to learn new skills, such as walking, feeding, and dressing themselves.

Preschoolers are fast becoming independent in many self-help skills, and need the opportunity to develop their interest in the world around them, which they will eagerly explore if we give them the encouragement and loving support to do so.

Starting school is a major developmental milestone. You can show your love for your school-age child by being interested in what they do at school, valuing their work, and supporting them in meeting the demands placed on them at school. Also do whatever you can to be part of your child's life at school, perhaps by being available to take children on class trips or camps from time to time.

Because the development of social skills is a very import-ant part of school life, encourage your child to invite friends home to play and perhaps to stay overnight. Provide what-ever opportunities you can for your child to develop skills in areas such as sport, music, and drama, without apply-ing any pressure.

The point I am making is that we demonstrate our love for our children not just with embraces, words of affection, and caring for their immediate physical needs, but also by helping them along the road to independence.

Teenagers

One way to show teenagers that they are loved is by gradu-ally giving them more and more responsibility for making their own decisions. By doing this we demonstrate our respect for their developing individuality, and we treat them more like the young adults they will soon be.

Give your teenagers increasing freedom to make choices on those issues which affect them, such as the style of clothes they wear, how they spend their money, and who their friends will be, while reserving the right to step in if they are acting in clearly risky or self-destructive ways. Show them how to make responsible decisions by weighing up the likely consequences of the options available to them, while leaving the final choice, as much as possible, over to them.

To love your teenager also means to be a good listener. As teenagers try to cope with their developing sexuality, pressure to perform at school, and worries about their future, they don't need advice and criticism so much as someone who will really listen to them.

Listening to your teenagers in a supportive and non-judgemental way gives them the chance to work through issues for themselves. Because listening is such an important skill, apparently simple but actually quite difficult to put into practice effectively, I have devoted an entire chapter to the subject later in the book (Chapter 5).

Even though teenagers are striving for their independence, they still need support and love in coping with the many new life-tasks they are expected to master. This usually happens at a time when both parents are fully involved with their own jobs, and perhaps thinking that their youngsters no longer need them as much as they did when they were little. This is a mistake. Your teenager may not need so much of your time, or be as dependent on you as during the early- and middle-childhood years, but your concern and availability are still vital. Teenagers can interpret your lack of availability as a lack of caring, which can not only cause deep hurt but may also lead to self-destructive behaviour.

It can take an immense amount of patience and self-restraint to perform the balancing act of not interfering too much in a teenager's life, while still having to set limits and lay down the law from time to time, but it is important that we try.

Cuddles

It goes almost without saying that the physical expression of our love for our children is very important, both for them and for ourselves. Holding, cuddling, and embracing our children is one of the simplest and greatest pleasures we can experience in life, and it is a direct and powerful way of showing that we care for them.

Cuddling little babies is irresistible for most parents, as well as for uncles, aunties, grannies, and passers-by! The softness, warmth, scent, and responsiveness of babies makes being close to them a very rewarding experience. It makes up for all the hard work they create for us, not to mention the torture of sleep deprivation! As they grow older and are able to embrace us in return, the pleasure becomes even greater, and we begin to think that maybe this parenting business is not so bad after all.

Unfortunately, as children grow into teenagers, they are usually not so keen for hugs with mum and dad. Even so, try to maintain as much physical contact as they will allow, even if it's only an arm around the shoulders.

It is a fact that some children don't like being cuddled. From babyhood they seem unresponsive to physical contact, and as they get older may seek to avoid it, wriggling like eels to escape any kind of embrace. This is a great pity for the parents, but will probably do the child no great harm. It is best understood as something inborn, something in the child's temperament. If you have a child like this, give as much physical affection as they will tolerate, and don't put yourself through the third degree to find out what you might have done to cause it, because it will be a futile search.

Non-cuddly children probably grow up to be non-cuddly parents. If you are one of these, once again don't worry too much about it. If something in your temperament or upbringing makes it difficult for you to be physically affectionate with your child, just do as much as you can without breaking into a sweat! If a hand on the shoulder or tousling the hair is as much as you can manage, do that with a smile and kind word — an occasional, genuine gesture like this from you will probably be treasured as much as a bear hug and smooch from a more expressive parent.

Remember that as children grow older and begin to understand more about people, they become remarkably tolerant and accepting of their parents' little eccentricities — they love us in spite of ourselves!

'I Love You'

Words are also very important. It's sad to hear, as I some-times do, grown-ups who confide that their parents never told them that they loved them. This is usually said either with a hint of tears, or sad resignation. The sight of these adults becoming children again before my eyes, children feeling the pain that their parents did not seem to care enough for them simply to say 'I love you', has reinforced a very basic parenting lesson for me: *tell your children that you love them.*

Also tell them that you think they are great kids, prob-ably the greatest on the planet, if not the whole street! It may be hard for you to do this because of your own up-bringing or family background. You may say, 'Well, they know that I love them — I don't have to tell them.' Perhaps you have, in fact, made it very clear to your children by what you do, that you value them and love them, but be on the safe side. We can never hear those three little words too often.

Consider this story. James was a nine-year-old boy whose defiant behaviour was causing major problems both at home and at school. I was sitting with his mother, Susan, in my office as we discussed the difficulties she and her husband were having with James.

When parents have serious problems in managing their children's behaviour over a long period of time, they can get to the point of actually not liking their children very much. This can create a vicious circle; the children pick up on their parents' negative feelings, which makes their behaviour worse, which upsets the parents even more, and so on. In situations such as this, I often ask parents directly if they like their child.

'It's very hard sometimes,' Susan answered, 'and I guess, to be honest, there are times when I really don't like him very much.'

'Do you tell him how you feel?'

'Yes. I tell him that it's hard for me to like him when he behaves the way he does, but that no matter what happens, I will always love him.'

Susan looked down for a minute, and there were tears welling up in her eyes as she continued.

'My parents never told me that they loved me. Never. They were kind to me, but for some reason found it hard to say anything positive about me, so I made up my mind that when I had children, I would make a point of telling them that I loved them. Sure, there are plenty of times when James makes me angry, and I tell him so, but not too many days go by without him hearing me say that I love him.'

Unconditional Love

At the beginning of this chapter I mentioned that our love for our children should be unconditional. Unconditional love is freely given, without strings or conditions attached. Some parents use their love as a way of controlling their children. Affection is given when the child's behaviour pleases the parent, but withheld when it does not. Because children have a strong need for their parents' approval and love, this can be a very powerful and effective method of controlling their behaviour, but it can have serious effects not only on a child's developing self-worth, but also on their sense of basic security.

If children feel they must do the 'right' thing in order to be loved, they live with uncertainty, always unsure whether their emotional lifeline will be yanked away if they break the rules. This not only makes them emotion- ally dependent on their parents, but also makes it very difficult for them to establish their own set of values and become individuals in their own right, even as adults, because they retain a lingering fear of going against their parents' wishes. Parents who use withdrawal of love as a control technique are seriously jeopardizing their children's chances of growing into emotionally mature, independent, and confident adults.

Reassure your child that even though you may sometimes growl at them and punish them, it is just their behaviour which annoys you — being angry with them doesn't mean that you don't love them.

In Summary

The message of this chapter is not just that it is important to love our children, which we all know, but it is essential for their self-esteem to know and feel that they are loved. Without this, they will find it very hard to develop a strong sense of self-worth, regardless of whatever else they might achieve in life. There are many apparently successful adults whose seeming confidence is only a brittle shell; at heart they are still vulnerable children, lacking in true self-esteem because they were never sure of their parents' love.

I am not suggesting that we should swamp our children with caresses and affection, or make them the very centre of our world. We need only to assure them through our words and actions that they are cared for and valued. If we do that we are laying the strong and stable foundation upon which a secure sense of self-worth can be built.

In this chapter I have also touched on themes which will be repeated and emphasized throughout the book: the importance for self-esteem of encouraging our children towards independence, of giving them the opportunity to make responsible choices, and of being a good listener.

3

Respect

Respect is an important ingredient of genuine love. If we truly love and care for our children there will be an element of respect in the way we respond to them. By respect I mean being able to see past the fact that they are our own children and being aware of their uniqueness and rights as totally separate, developing human beings and individuals. This attitude is the direct opposite of the belief that children are somehow the property of their parents, to be treated as the parents see fit.

In the day-to-day business of parenting, respect for our children's individuality cannot be our first, or even a frequent, response, but we certainly need to think about it from time to time. If we have an attitude of fundamental respect for our children, it will be conveyed to them in subtle ways that eventually will have a significant, positive effect on their self-esteem.

Children's Rights

At a minimal level, we demonstrate respect for our children by providing for their basic physical needs, protecting them from danger and illness, and not subjecting them to any form of deliberate abuse, whether physical or mental. In most families and societies today, these things can be taken for granted. It is only when families, or societies, become seriously disordered that children are ignored, harmed, or exploited.

If children's basic rights to nurture and protection are not being met within a family, it is a sign that, for whatever reason, the family's functioning has broken down disastrously. In most Western countries, children now have legal protection against abuse and exploitation, and agencies exist to provide help in cases of serious neglect; even in prosperous societies many children are still deprived of even minimal care and protection.

Ideally, respecting our children means more than just acknowledging their right to have their basic needs met. It means recognizing them as young people with their own personalities and potential. In the hurly-burly of family life we may often overlook the fact that our children are developing individuals who happen to be under our guardianship. As their guardians, it is our role and responsibility to protect and nurture their uniqueness.

Listening

We can show our respect for children at different stages of their development simply by listening to them. For example, we help toddlers to develop their language skills by taking the trouble to listen to their early attempts at speech, giving them the time and encouragement to express what they want to say, and by responding to them.

As our children master the mechanics of speech and the basics of language, the messages they give us provide an insight into how they see the world. As they explore, think about, and experiment with their environment, it is important to respond to the comments they make and the questions they ask, because in this way we promote their intellectual development.

On the other hand, because young children tend to express their thoughts and feelings as soon as they come to mind, we can become submerged in a sea of chatter.

Our defence mechanism in these situations tends to be an automatic 'Oh, really?' or 'That's nice!'

There is no way we can give full attention to our toddlers and preschoolers whenever they want it, but from time to time we need to respect them sufficiently to give them our undivided attention, really listen, and respond to their questions and comments as thoughtfully as we can. As our children get older, this is the way we help them to formulate their values, beliefs, and attitudes.

The compensation for the parental effort involved is that the opinions of older children become more interesting. An exchange of views with a ten-year-old about the rights and wrongs of something can be both absorbing and challenging. Really listening to teenagers' views on contraception or a career choice can certainly be challenging, but could also have a vital effect on the choices and decisions they will make. We need to respect teenagers enough to hear them out, even though their opinions may differ from ours.

Talking *with* Children

If you think about the ways we communicate with children, most of what we say to them is in the form of requests, commands, directions, or questions. We seldom address comments, observations, or statements about how we feel to our children (other than annoyance perhaps!). This is understandable when they are very young, but as they reach late primary-school age, we should sometimes try to share our feelings and opinions with them. This could be on such topics as our favourite foods, something interesting we've read in the paper or seen on television, or an experience we had as a child. When we do this, the implication is that we respect our children enough to share our opinions and feelings with them.

Telling your child about something that happened to you today, or sharing a childhood memory, whether pleasant or unpleasant, can create an atmosphere of real closeness between you. It can sometimes also help your child to deal with issues of a similar nature which she or he has been reluctant to tell you about, or give your child the confidence to raise a problem with you directly and ask for your advice.

We also need to think about *how* we speak to our children. We convey a message of respect in simple, daily acts of politeness, such as a friendly greeting, the use of 'please' and 'thank you', apologizing when we are in the wrong, and asking permission before we use things belonging to them.

Time

Time with our children is the foundation for everything we would like to achieve as parents. By doing things with them we give our children the unspoken message that we value them enough to spend time with them, even though there are lots of other things needing to be done or, to be honest, that we would rather be doing.

Children whose parents make an effort to do things with them right through their childhood are much less likely to become involved later in the kinds of activities that most parents worry about. This is partly because the more interaction we have with our children the more likely they are to absorb our values. It is also because children who feel valued and respected by their parents are more likely to have a stronger sense of self-esteem, and so are less likely to seek the approval of their peers by taking part in risky or illicit activities.

Family Meetings

An important way in which we show respect for our children as they grow older is by asking for their opinion on important family decisions. This can be done from early primary-school age as part of the very useful system of having regular family meetings, perhaps after a meal on a day when people don't have to rush off to do other things.

Family meetings are a time to discuss those matters that are causing concern or frustration among family members, whether parents or children. Any issues that can be dealt with by open discussion leading to an agreed plan of action are suitable for a family meeting. Such issues could be: what can be done about the family dog not being taken for a walk regularly; whether the family should move house; where to go for a holiday; or how to stop the constant bickering between two of the children.

Here's an example of how a family meeting might go. The Thompson family had finished their evening meal. Once the table had been cleared they sat down again.

'What are we going to talk about tonight?' asked seven-year-old Michael.

'Well,' said Mrs Thompson, 'your father and I thought we should get your ideas on what we can do to make sure that the dog is taken for walks regularly. It seems he's only being taken about once a week these days, and that isn't really enough. When we got him, we agreed that you children would have the responsibility of looking after him.'

'I've tried taking him for walks,' said Michael, 'but he's so big I can't control him sometimes, especially when we go past the house down the street where the other dog lives.'

'So you feel he's a bit much for you to handle?'

'Yeah, I guess so, Mum.'

'What are your thoughts, Sarah?' her father asked.

'Well, I don't mind taking him for a walk, but I don't want to have to do it every day.'

'OK guys, so what are we going to do about this?' asked Mr Thompson.

For the next ten minutes or so the family discussed the problems, possibilities, and practicalities of making sure that the dog was taken for a walk regularly. The children's ideas, comments, and objections were listened to. In the end, a workable solution was arrived at, with an agreement to look at it after a few weeks to see how it was going.

'Thanks for your help on that one, kids,' said Mrs Thompson. 'Now, what's on TV tonight? Anything we can all watch?'

Even more important than the solution here, however, was the process for reaching it. Apart from the fact that this kind of open discussion with a problem-solving focus can often lead to a solution, the implied message to the children who take part is that their opinions are valued and respected. This can have subtle but real benefits for their self-concept and confidence.

Trust

Respect and trust go hand in hand. We show respect for our children by trusting them to do the right thing, to be responsible, and by believing in their inborn desire to become independent and self-sufficient. By doing this we actually increase the chances that they will behave independently and responsibly, because children tend to behave as we expect them to.

It works the other way, too. When children misbehave, we can lose our confidence in their ability to behave sensibly and reasonably. This feeling, even though we may not say anything directly, can show itself in an expectation that they will behave badly in certain situations. Such an expectation has a way of communicating itself to children, who then live up to it. Once we have dealt with misbehaviour, we should give youngsters the chance to show that they are capable of behaving appropriately by wiping the slate clean, starting afresh each day, and trusting them to do the right thing.

When children are learning a new skill, we need to give them as much instruction and encouragement as we can, but then we have to trust in their ability to do the rest for themselves. Learning to ride a bike is a good example; there comes a point when we have to let go and allow the laws of physics to take over, hoping that momentum will triumph over gravity! Probably the teenage years are the most difficult time for parents to keep faith with this principle. It is then that we must rely on all our years of love, training, and support to bear fruit, as our young people face difficult and risky decisions in regard to choice of friends, the use of drugs, sexual behaviour, staying at school, and career.

As teenagers approach young adulthood, they still need our support and advice. If we have built up a relationship of trust and respect with them, they will be able to ask us for help if they need it. But in the end the choices are theirs alone to make, and the consequences theirs to live with. If we continue to show our trust in their ability to make the right choice for *them*, even if it is not the one we would like to see, we build up their confidence in their own abilities and give them the chance to make a choice free from emotional pressure.

When we trust our children to do the right thing, and show our confidence in them, we provide the circumstances for them to grow to their potential with a strong and healthy sense of their own abilities and worth. And that's what self-esteem is all about.

Respecting Individuality

Both common experience and research tell us that all children are born as unique individuals. Children in the same family develop different personalities, despite the fact that the same child-rearing methods are used for each of them. Some children seem to be stubborn and temperamental from babyhood, while others are placid, responsive, and easygoing.

Intensive study of newborn babies has confirmed the experience of parents. When babies are assessed on such aspects as their response to stimuli like light and noise, the regularity of their feeding and sleeping cycles, activity level, and overall mood, there are clear individual differences. Even before the effects of parenting begin to mould a child's personality, a basic structure is already there.

Children are also born with individual strengths and weaknesses. For some, excellent physical co-ordination means that running, climbing, and riding are mastered quickly and easily. As these children become older, they may excel in a range of sports. For others, drawing, music, or practical construction-type activities are areas where they show particular talent and interest. Some children's verbal abilities are excellent from an early age, often associated with the easy acquisition of reading and writing skills. On the other hand, some children are physically unco-ordinated and clumsy, and for them it can be a painful process to learn to ride a bike, kick a ball, or swim. Others find it hard to sing in tune, draw more than a stick man, or learn to read and write.

My experience has led me to conclude that all children have a unique profile of skills and abilities, a pattern of highs and lows, which is theirs alone. Our job as parents is to be aware of that pattern, to encourage the development of potential strengths, and to accept that our children may probably always find some skills difficult to master. It can be very hard to accept that our children may not ever achieve success in areas that are important to us, or to society. Our task is then to search for the strengths which will undoubtedly be there if only we look.

If we know and respect our children's individuality, and if we give them the opportunity and encouragement to develop whatever talents they may have, we will inevitably help the growth of their self-esteem.

In Summary

It is of course important for children to respect their parents — I certainly do not dispute that. I think it is equally important, however, that there should be a dimension of respect for children in our parenting, and that from time to time we focus on our role as guardians of their developing uniqueness. If we show respect for our children by listening to them, talking with them, trusting them to do the right thing, and simply being with them, we will be helping them to forge a strong, positive self-concept.

4

Independence

Our bottom-line responsibility as parents is to prepare our children for ultimate independence. We have done our job properly when our children leave the nest prepared to establish their own lives as well-adjusted, confident adults.

Independence and self-esteem are closely interrelated. As we master the tasks which life presents, we see ourselves more positively. As we learn new skills, we become more confident, less dependent on others, and our sense of self-worth increases.

The Drive to Learn New Skills

The job of helping our children towards independence begins in the earliest years. Children have a natural and strong desire to do things for themselves. All we have to do is foster and encourage that desire, giving them the opportunities and support they need to master new skills. Just look at the determination of babies learning to reach out, roll over, crawl, and walk. We need to be there to look after their safety, but the drive to do these things comes from within themselves.

At the toddler stage we can help our children to become independent in what are known as self-help skills. For example, they can begin to learn to undress themselves by starting with the things that are easy to remove, such as socks, knickers, and jackets. We can allow toddlers the chance to feed themselves, in spite of our worries about a

Doing things for herself.

major mess, by splash-proofing part of the dining area and by giving them the right tools and enough time to do the job. Toddlers can also learn, under our watchful guidance, to help to wash themselves in the bath.

In all these efforts it is usually the lack of time that sabotages our best intentions. Toddlers have their own priorities and time-scale for doing things, which, unfortunately, seldom match up with our own. If you decide to let baby try to do something for her- or himself, make sure you don't do it at a time when you are in a rush to get ready, otherwise you will become impatient, baby will get upset, and the experience will be mutually frustrating rather than rewarding.

To avoid this scenario, we often end up doing things for our children as a matter of course. We need to be realistic and accept that, as we rush to meet all the deadlines associated with raising a young family, not every task in a toddler's day can be turned into an opportunity to learn a new skill. On the other hand, we shouldn't automatically do everything for them. It can be hard to see children struggling to master something new, and being frustrated when the demands of the task are slightly beyond their skills. Sometimes we will step in and help, but we must give our children the chance to master new skills for themselves. Not only do they need this chance, but the obvious satisfaction they gain from the experience is just as rewarding for us as parents.

Today's Families

For today's families, many factors work against providing children with opportunities to develop self-reliance. For a start, families today are generally smaller. In the days when large families were common, children had to learn to do things for themselves because there simply wasn't enough parent time to go around. Children also had responsibility from an early age to carry out the chores that are essential for a large family's day-to-day survival.

Secondly, whereas families of a few generations ago had to be self-reliant in providing for the necessities and comforts of life, today's children have much less required of them in a household. Whatever they need can usually be provided by the flick of a switch or a drive to the nearest shop. For example, they aren't expected to create their own toys by using a bit of imagination, cardboard boxes, and Sellotape. The availability of plastic toys inspired by the latest popular movie or television series denies children the chance to create and craft playthings for themselves, and to experience the power of their own imagination.

Thirdly, there is the real problem of danger. Because of the risks on the roads with fast traffic, and the slight but worrying chance of harm from adults who prey on children, many parents are now reluctant to let their children do the things which didn't cause parents a second thought twenty or thirty years ago — simple activities, such as riding a bike around the neighbourhood, walking to the local shops, or walking alone to school. Parents now have to hesitate over and think carefully about whether their children can do these things safely, and some decide that they cannot. This means, of course, that children now have fewer opportunities for those natural, spontaneous learning experiences that extend their skills in small but important ways, and help them to grow almost imperceptibly in self-confidence.

From my observations, the balance has probably tipped a little too far in the direction of caution, and we have become too protective of our children. It actually does them no harm to walk half a mile or so to school, and even to walk there in the rain, provided they have the right clothing and footwear. And what about the pleasure of taking shoes and socks off and splashing in a puddle or squelching in some mud? If we shelter children too much from natural experiences of fatigue, cold, rain, and dirt, and if we deny them the chance to encounter a little discomfort, how will they cope with some of the major problems that life has in store for most of us?

Discomfort, disappointment, and frustration are part of life for us on this planet. Modern society shields us from much of it, but as a result we are beginning to expect that there is a technological solution to all the problems we experience. Unfortunately, this is not the case. We need to allow our children the chance to confront and overcome little obstacles and discomforts, so that they gradually build up confidence in their ability to deal with them on their own.

We also need to be careful not to inflict our own fears and phobias on our children. There may be situations or activities that make us unreasonably anxious or afraid. We owe it to our children not to infect them with our fear, or deny them the chance to take part in activities which make us nervous but which they enjoy.

Sport and Other Activities

Sport is probably one of the few areas left in many children's lives where they can experience the challenge of a demanding and sometimes physically risky activity, find out about not giving in when the going gets tough, and literally learn to be brave. There are all kinds of situations in sport and outdoor activities where young people have the chance to face a challenge, overcome it, and experience the powerful satisfaction of doing something difficult.

During the primary-school years it's a good idea to give children the chance to take part in a range of sports and outdoor activities, so that by the time they are teenagers they have become interested in and have mastered a few of them. Busy teenagers who are fully involved in school and sport have less opportunity, or need, to take part in dangerous or self-destructive activities, such as taking drugs. Teenagers who experience the natural highs of sporting achievement — not only the enjoyment of mastering difficult skills but also the excitement of occasional victory — have less need to seek the chemical highs of alcohol and other drugs.

It is also widely acknowledged that drug use and other illegal activities among teenagers are often associated with low self-esteem. Boosting children's self-esteem in their younger years by providing them with opportunities to become independent, self-reliant, and successfully involved in a range of activities, is a good insurance policy against tears and trouble in the teenage years.

Here's an example of the kind of situation that occurs almost daily in most families, which can be used by parents either to maintain dependence, or encourage independence:

'Dad, I've got a project to do on dinosaurs and we don't have any books about them. Will you take me to the library?'

'Sure, Sam — how about Saturday morning?'

When nine-year-old Sam and his dad arrived at the library that Saturday, Sam asked: 'Will you find me some books, Dad?'

'Well, Sam, I think it would be better if you looked for them yourself. You'll be getting lots of school projects to do in the next few years. Finding out how to use the library will be a good skill for you to learn.'

'But I don't know where to look.'

'Tell you what. Why don't you go and ask the librarian over there what to do?'

'Me?'

'Yes, you!'

It took a bit of encouragement, but Sam eventually went up to the librarian by himself and told her what he wanted. She then took him over to the computer index, showed him how to use it, and explained where to find the books he was interested in. Shortly afterwards Sam and his dad were coming down the library steps with an armful of books each.

'Hey, Dad, I did it,' said Sam with a proud grin.

'You sure did, Sam. You sure did!'

Children's self-worth is related to the degree of control they feel they have over their own lives. If we encourage and support our children towards self-reliance in the daily activities of life — from dressing and feeding in the early years to making responsible choices as teenagers — they begin to see themselves as competent individuals. Then their response to challenges is likely to be a confident 'I can do this', rather than 'Who will do this for me?'

The old belief is still valid and relevant today, that our character is shaped by the way we respond to difficulties. In the language of psychology, if we want our children to develop a response tendency of approach rather than avoidance when they encounter a problem, then we should expose them gradually to a widening range of new tasks to be mastered. As their competence grows, so will their self-confidence.

Think about it right now. What are the things you are still doing for your child that she or he could do alone? For the sake of your child's self-esteem, isn't it time you stood back and let them get on with it themselves?

5

Listening

Being a good listener is a parenting skill which can have major benefits for your family. In particular, being listened to can help in the development of your child's sense of self-worth. By listening actively and attentively to children you give them the important message that you respect and care for them enough to hear what they have to say. In addition, active listening is an excellent way to help children resolve for themselves some of the daily problems they have to deal with, whether minor or major. For both these reasons, it is worth spending a little time learning how to be an effective listener.

Listening seems to be a simple skill to acquire, but to do it properly, in fact, takes a little practice and requires some self-control. This is because the most important part of the listening process doesn't come naturally.

Feelings

Family life is based on feelings. In the family we try to meet our needs for love, support, security, and belonging. However, because other family members are sometimes unable to satisfy these needs for us, and because just living with other people usually brings with it an interesting variety of frustrations and annoyances, emotions in families can sometimes run high. When these feelings are expressed, our natural response is to react or respond to the content of what is said. For example, children often say things like:

- 'You're always picking on me.'
- 'I hate you.'
- 'You're mean.'
- 'How come you never make Jason pick up his toys?'

When we hear such comments, our natural tendency as parents is to respond with denial, disbelief, dismissal, or a mountain of evidence to convince the child that they are not just wrong but seriously deluded. What we usually do is respond with everything but a simple acceptance of the feeling behind the statement, such as:

- 'You're really feeling pretty angry with me, aren't you?'
- 'You really don't like me right now, do you?'
- 'You don't think I'm being very fair?'
- 'You think I let Jason get away with things, don't you?'

If your child is making an obviously strongly felt statement, it can help to focus on the feeling and acknowledge it. The effect of doing this can sometimes be almost miraculous. If your child feels that they are really being listened to and taken seriously, they can let off steam quickly, and the actual problem can then be seen more clearly and objectively. In fact, once the emotional steam has been released, the problem often seems to be reduced to a manageable size.

If, however, the feeling is *not* heard and acknowledged, then frustration is added to the original problem, leading to further tension and a breakdown in communication.

Active Listening

Although 'active' listening, as it is often called, can sometimes be dramatically effective, it takes effort on the part of the listener to do it properly. For example, let's say that your ten-year-old daughter is lying on her bed, obviously grumpy. You ask what the problem is and she says, 'You

took David to the supermarket with you after school, and
he got a chocolate! You never take me to the supermarket!'

You now have two choices. You can either try to convince your daughter by using faultless reasoning, relent-
less logic, and overwhelming evidence that in fact she does
often come to the supermarket with you, that she wasn't
around when it was time to go, that you took her shop-
ping with you when David was at soccer on Saturday and
bought her some jellybeans, and so on. All of this is most
unlikely to convince her that her grievance is unreasonable, because reason, logic, and weight of evidence don't
stack up against feeling.

It is the feeling that must be dealt with before the facts
can be looked at. If the feelings are dealt with properly, the
so-called problem may just disappear. If, instead of trying
to argue her out of her mood, you respond to it with active
listening, the dialogue might go something like this:

'So, you're pretty mad with me?'

'Yeah, I am!'

'You think it's not fair that I took David to the supermarket without you?'

'Yeah. I was really mad when I found out ... I felt left
out. Just because he's younger than me, he gets all the
good things.'

'You think he gets good things and you don't?'

'And he gets away with things because he's little ... he
teases me, and if I do anything to him you tell me off and
not him.'

'Sounds to me like there's a few things you're upset
about.'

'Yeah. If you could realize that just because David's
the youngest he shouldn't get away with things. If David
and I are having a fight, it's not always my fault.'

'OK, I'll try!'

(Pause, then quietly) 'Thanks, Mum.'

In this example, the real issue to emerge was one of

fairness. The daughter felt that because her brother was little, he was getting away with things. Not going to the supermarket was really only a minor problem which represented a reservoir of resentment growing from her perception that she was being treated unfairly. Trying to deal with the supermarket incident on its own by reason and persuasion would probably have led only to mutual exasperation with the daughter in tears, her mother storming out in a temper, and nothing resolved.

Now that the daughter has been able to express her feelings without having to justify or defend them, they will lose some of their power, and there is a much greater chance that she and her mother will be able to work out some kind of solution to the problem. At the very least, her mother now has a greater understanding of why her daughter's emotional reactions sometimes seem out of proportion to the incident.

The Essential Ingredients of Active Listening

Active listening can be used with all children from pre-schoolers upwards. The essential procedure is to:

- Identify the feeling behind the statement,
- Focus on the feeling, and
- Follow the feeling as the dialogue proceeds.

This interaction with your child is best done by reflecting the feelings which you pick up, in your own words. Examples of such an exchange might be:

- 'I hate David!'
  'You're feeling pretty angry with him, then?'
- 'Mrs Thomas was really mean to me today.'
  'Sounds like you're upset about that.'
- 'I don't want to go down to my room in the dark.'
  'You're feeling a bit scared about it, are you?'

Listening is not just an attitude of mind.

It will feel awkward and funny at first to talk like this, but if you concentrate on the feelings that your child is trying to express, and do your best to reflect them, it will soon begin to seem natural. If it's not clear what the underlying feeling is, it's OK to say something like, 'I'm trying to understand what you're feeling at the moment, but I can't quite get it.' Your child will soon clarify the picture for you.

Not all situations need this kind of response, of course. When your child says, 'Mum, I can't find my socks', there's no need to say meaningfully, 'So, you're feeling pretty frustrated about that?' Just telling him that they're in the wash will do! Don't think that you should try to turn every statement of feeling from your child into a kind of mini counselling session.

Good listening is not just an attitude of mind — it is also a physical attitude. We show that we are really listening as much by our posture as by our words. We need to:

- Stop what we are doing;
- Turn towards the child;
- Look at them directly; and
- Get down to their level if necessary.

This physical part of being a good listener is known as attending. Your child won't be convinced that you are taking them seriously if you keep on reading the paper while they speak. If you decide that this is the time for really listening to what they have to say, do it properly. If a genuinely important issue has come up and you can't stop what you are doing right at that moment, tell your child so. Then say when you *will* be able to talk and give your full attention.

Listening and Self-esteem

Being a good listener can bring major benefits to a family. It can defuse tensions by allowing children to express their feelings rather than keep the lid on them. It demonstrates clearly that you respect and care enough for your child to really be with them, to focus on their world as they themselves are experiencing it. Not only will this bolster their self-esteem, but it will bring you closer together as a family.

Feelings are the foundation of being human, the heart and soul of family life. Helping our children to understand, express, and cope with their emotions is one of the most useful things we can do as parents. We can show them that feelings have control over us only so long as we keep them suppressed and simmering inside. Once they are spoken, acknowledged, and discussed without criticism or judgement, much of their ability to influence our behaviour disappears.

When children and young people express their feelings to an attentive listener, it helps them to:

- Reduce issues which may seem overwhelming down to a manageable size;
- Better understand the nature, power, and importance of our emotions;
- Learn more about who they are as individuals; and
- Learn that it is OK to express feelings, and that once a feeling is expressed, it can be dealt with.

All of these outcomes will have a positive effect on young people's self-esteem because they enhance their self-knowledge, their sense of self-control, and their confidence to cope with everyday problems.

Start with the Positive

As I mentioned before, it is not easy to learn the skill of active or reflective listening. As with any new skill, it takes effort and practice to get it right. Our first attempts may feel awkward, and we have to work hard to avoid giving our usual responses of:

- Disagreeing;
- Arguing;
- Persuading;
- Judging;
- Interrogating;
- Moralizing; or
- Lecturing,

rather than simply listening with our full attention, then reflecting back the feeling content of what we have heard.

Rather than starting with the more difficult emotions of sadness or anger, you might find it helpful to begin practising your listening skills with positive feelings such as happiness, pride, and satisfaction:

- 'Sounds like you had a good day at school today.'
- 'You look pretty happy about the way you played in the second half.'
- 'Seems like you're quite pleased with that drawing.'

Keep the conversation going with open-ended questions, such as, 'How did you feel when that happened?', 'What did you think about that?', or 'Then what happened?' rather than:

- 'You shouldn't have ... '
- 'Why didn't you ... '
- 'I've told you not to ... '
- 'What you should have done was ... '
- 'I remember when I was your age ... '
- 'Well, that was a silly thing to do ... '

Such statements are just about guaranteed to stop any expression of real feeling from children, and close them down into defensive mode. Practising with positive, low-key, non-threatening situations makes it less likely that this will happen, and will help you to become comfortable with the technique before trying it in more stressful situations where you would really like to help your child (and yourself) to work through a difficult emotion.

In Summary

Active listening is an apparently simple but very useful technique with great potential for improving family communication and relationships. It involves:

- Focusing our whole attention on the person we are listening to;
- Working hard to understand what they are feeling and experiencing;
- Expressing that understanding as best we can by reflecting back what we have heard and understood; and
- Avoiding judgement, criticism, argument, or advice.

Active listening helps us to deal with the unspoken emotions that drive many family conflicts. This is especially so if we can sometimes accept the expression of negative feelings or criticism from our children without becoming angry or judgemental, seeing this as part of a problem-solving process.

For parents, listening is a very practical way to express love and respect for their children. It has major beneficial side-effects for children's self-esteem, and also helps them to understand more about and control their own feelings.

6

Parenting Style

Each of us has an individual parenting style which is a reflection of the kind of person we are. It is influenced by all the factors that make us unique, including our upbringing, our personality, and our values. Each of these factors affects how we see our role as parents, how we behave towards our children, and what we expect of them.

Our parenting style has a direct effect on our children's self-esteem because it determines the character of our day-to-day relationship with them. Many of our interactions with our children have the potential to affect their self-esteem, either positively or negatively, depending on how we respond. In this chapter we look at various aspects of parenting style, including our values, standards, expectations, and how we exercise control over our children.

Values and Behavioural Standards

Our values are our beliefs about what is good and bad, right and wrong. They have a major influence on our parenting because we naturally encourage our children to behave according to the standards we believe in. It's important to be as clear as we can about what our basic values actually are. If we are clear about them in our minds, it makes our parenting task easier because we can then set definite behavioural guidelines for our children, which helps us to be consistent in our expectations.

Having clear standards also makes it easier for children

to monitor and control their own behaviour, for a number of reasons. Firstly, young children actually prefer to have behavioural boundaries because it helps them to structure their world and make sense of it, giving them a sense of security. Secondly, human behaviour is also partly guided and controlled by 'self-talk' — what we say to ourselves when we are thinking about how we should behave in a particular situation.

For young children, it is helpful for them to have a set of ready-made statements which they can play back to themselves when they are at the point of deciding how they should behave, such as: 'It's not right to take things that don't belong to you', 'It's good to share your toys', or 'We don't swear in this family.'

Older preschoolers and young primary-school children go through a stage when such rules are seen as having great power, and they will say things like, 'We're not allowed to ... ', 'Mum said we had to ... ', or 'The teacher said we couldn't ... ', as if these were immutable laws of the universe. Parents should take advantage of this stage of being receptive to behavioural guidelines by having them ready, and using them frequently.

There's no need to have rules enough to fill a book, however. It's better to have a small number that are really important to you, express your basic values, and are likely to apply to a wide range of situations. This way your children will more easily internalize them as their own personal code of conduct. Not only will this give them the feeling that the world is orderly and predictable, but it increases the chances that they will do the right thing and so gain the powerful reward of your approval. Most children feel better about themselves if their good behaviour is noticed, and praised.

I don't mean that you should run your home like a military base, with rules posted, medals for good conduct, and time in solitary confinement for disobeying orders.

This kind of authoritarian approach may produce effective soldiers, but, as we shall see later in the chapter, it has major weaknesses as a method of child-rearing. I do think it is useful, however, to spend some time thinking about and clarifying your values, how you see your role as a parent, and the goals you have for your child's development. In all these things, if you can describe them in terms of specific behaviours, you are more likely to achieve them. The benefits for your child's self-confidence and self-esteem will be:

- The security of a home environment which has structure and predictability; and
- The opportunity for your child to feel good about herself or himself by being able to meet your clear, consistent behavioural standards.

Know Yourself

Part of being a good parent is knowing yourself. We are individuals and people first, before we are parents. It is inevitable that our background and personality will affect the way we behave towards our children. This is not necessarily a bad thing, of course, but it can be if our parenting philosophy is a reaction to our own childhood experiences rather than an expression of our personal values and beliefs. An example of this is a parent who told me that she was very permissive with her daughter because her own parents had been so strict with her that she had vowed never to behave like that towards her own children. More often, however, the effect of our own upbringing works at a less conscious level.

If we can look objectively at our behaviour as parents we may find that some of our attitudes or expectations are in fact unreasonable. This may be because, although we are unaware of it, they derive in some way from our own childhood experiences, or from slightly neurotic aspects of our personality (which we all have!). An example is the father who believes that he shouldn't show physical affection to a son, or that boys should behave in a stereotyped male fashion. Some parents place excessive importance on high academic achievement, or winning at all costs. Some are very anxious about granting their children independence, and letting them do slightly risky things.

We need to look at our behaviour as parents from time to time, and ask for our partner's perspective, because we may be placing pressure on our children to do things that are unnecessary, or stressful, or that don't suit their personalities. If we do this we may harm their self-esteem because they are unable to meet what, in fact, are unrealistic expectations. They may grow up feeling that whatever they do, it is never quite good enough.

If you want to check for aspects of your parenting that may be slightly irrational or unrealistic, and that may be placing unnecessary stress on your child, be aware of those things your child does which make you particularly irritable, angry, or worried. Then ask yourself if your emotional reaction is in proportion to what your child has actually done. If it isn't, then the emotion may be coming from unresolved issues in your own childhood, or tender spots in your own personality, which you need to deal with. This is much more easily said than done, but awareness of these emotional 'buttons' may help you to control your response if your child unwittingly presses one.

Control and Discipline

The research on child development has established very clearly that the way parents exercise power in the home has a marked effect on children's behaviour. Parenting styles can be analysed according to the kind of control that parents exercise over their children — authoritarian, permissive, or democratic. To put it another way, families differ in how they share power.

Authoritarian Parenting

In some families one parent, often the father, holds the reins. He makes most of the major decisions about what happens in the family, often without consulting other family members, and his wishes and preferences are deferred to by both his wife and children, usually without question. In such families, the day-to-day relationship between parents and children is based on the use of power, and children simply do as they are told. If they don't, physical punishment may be the first response, even through to the teenage years.

The idea of listening to the opinion of children, or discussing family issues with them, is not readily accepted in such families. Communication from parents to children is often very directive and based on criticism for not following orders rather than praise and encouragement for behaving appropriately. This is one extreme of the parent control scale, a style which is usually called *authoritarian*, for obvious reasons. The power of the authoritarian parent is absolute. This style of parenting is reasonably common, partly because it is characteristic of a number of cultures where the father is the traditional head of the family.

It is not hard to imagine the effects on a child's self-esteem of growing up in an authoritarian home. It is difficult for children to develop a sense of self-confidence and self-worth if their feelings and opinions are usually ignored, if criticism and punishment are more common than praise and encouragement, and if they seldom have the chance to develop judgement or exercise responsibility.

Growing up in such a family can also have a significant effect on a child's moral development. Children are much more likely to grow up with an effective social conscience if they are able to discuss issues of right and wrong with their parents. But if they are usually directed what to do without explanation, and punished without right of appeal, they may grow up either submissive to authority or defiant. They will probably also have the idea that if they can escape punishment for breaking the rules, then breaking the rules is OK.

I met fourteen-year-old Mark in a social welfare boys' home. He had been sent there because of his increasing involvement with shoplifting, burglary, and glue-sniffing.

Mark had a thick file recording his contact over the years with social workers, psychologists, child-health professionals, and school counsellors. He had first come to social welfare attention as a toddler because of physical abuse. One of a large family, Mark had received lots of loving attention as a baby, but as he became older, more independent, and more demanding, he had been either left to amuse himself or shouted at and smacked if he got into mischief. Mark wasn't really getting into 'mischief', just being a normally active and curious toddler, but with such a large family his parents didn't have the energy or resources to spend time with him and provide him with suitable activities.

In Mark's family, decisions were made on the basis of power. His father was the undisputed head of the house and any arguing or disagreement from the children was dealt with sharply and harshly. Mark's mother was sometimes beaten as well. The idea of listening to or considering the children's opinions and feelings was almost unknown, and words of praise were seldom heard.

By the time Mark was about seven, boredom and resentment had driven him to seek companionship and excitement on the streets with his friends. They admired the older boys who defied and ignored their parents and got into trouble with the police. As Mark got older, a gang provided him with friendship and a sense of belonging, but even in this 'family' the use of physical force was always the bottom line.

Mark was, in fact, an intelligent boy, but school had never been valued by his parents and it held little interest for him. By the time he was in his early teens, he was truanting regularly.

Although it was not the only negative factor in his development, Mark's upbringing in an authoritarian family severely damaged his sense of self-esteem, limited his ability to reason and discuss issues, and left him with the moral development of a preschooler.

Permissive Parenting

At the other extreme of the control scale are parents who see children as being more or less their equals, and who are reluctant to exercise any kind of authority. In theory, family members share power equally and one person's wishes are no more important than anyone else's. Children are always asked for their opinions on what should happen in the family, and the main parenting rule seems to be, 'If the kids want to do it, that's OK.' This kind of parenting is called *permissive*, and is actually quite rare.

A different kind of permissive parenting occurs much more commonly when adults are unable or unwilling to exercise control over their children, either because they lack the personal resources to do so, or they are just not interested. This type of permissiveness is, in fact, neglect. It is usually not the result of deliberate choice on the parents' part, because it is often associated with poverty. The grinding stress of being poor can leave parents with little energy for their children, who end up ignored and unsupervised, with predictable results.

At the other end of the socio-economic scale, the children of wealthy parents can suffer the same fate, but for different reasons. Parents who are dedicated to acquiring and enjoying material wealth sometimes seem to think that money and possessions can substitute for their time, but of course this isn't so. The effects of neglect are the same, regardless of whether a family is poor or rich. Children who feel that their parents don't care enough to spend time with them, or get the impression that they are little more than a nuisance in their parents' lives, can become bitter and hardened towards them as they get older. When they reach the teenage years, they may get into serious trouble as a way of punishing their parents and expressing their hurt.

Democratic Parenting

In the middle of the parent power scale, where the majority of families come, is the kind of home where the parents share power reasonably equally, and the children have some say in decision-making. Other characteristics of this kind of home are:

- There are fairly clear standards for the children about what kind of behaviour is acceptable, and fairly consistent consequences for either meeting those standards or not.
- Parents are prepared to explain the reasons for their rules, and will listen to their children if they ask questions about them or feel they are being treated unfairly.
- Praise and reasoning are used as discipline techniques more often than criticism and punishment.
- Parents openly show their affection for their children.

This style of parenting is sometimes called *democratic* because the parents maintain a position of authority while allowing children to express their opinions, and encouraging dialogue on issues affecting the family. Implied in this approach are respect for children as individuals, and trust that they will respond to being given the chance to have some say in decisions that affect them.

The results of research are clear that the democratic parenting style has real benefits for children's development. Compared with the children of authoritarian or permissive parents, those brought up in a democratic home environment are more likely to be independent and self-reliant, and to have greater self-esteem. This is because they not only have the security of clear behaviour guidelines, but also the opportunity to reflect on them and discuss them, which develops their reasoning ability and the confidence to trust their own judgement. In a democratically run home there is respect for the rules, respect for the rights of the individual, and plenty of discussion.

In Summary

Our behaviour as parents has a direct effect on our children's self-esteem. Individual parenting style is based on our own upbringing, our personalities, and our values. It is helpful if we can think about and clarify our role as parents so that we can set clear behavioural standards for our children, and avoid having expectations of them that are unreasonable or unrealistic.

If we want our children to have a clear set of values to guide their behaviour in a positive way, we must give them the opportunity to think about issues of right and wrong, about why we have rules, and, especially, the effect that their behaviour has on other people. Young people who have gradually developed a social conscience in this way over their childhood and teenage years are much more likely to behave thoughtfully, sensibly, and responsibly when it matters.

Families differ in the way they share and exercise power, ranging on a control scale from authoritarian to permissive. The democratic parenting style, which comes midway on the scale, gives children freedom and responsibility within limits. The limits provide security, while freedom and responsibility provide the opportunity for children to become more self-reliant, and feel better about themselves as a result. From the point of view of developing self-esteem, independence, and moral judgement in children, the democratic parenting style is very effective.

7

Belonging

Human beings are clearly social creatures. From the moment of our birth we become members of an interlocking set of social groups beginning with our blood relatives and extending out in widening circles through community, nation, and race to the biggest group of them all: the human family.

It is important for our psychological health that we belong to at least one group where we feel valued as an individual. Being isolated and alone is normally experienced as unpleasant and undesirable. On the other hand, we can enhance our sense of well-being, and our self-concept, by belonging to and identifying with certain groups.

Families

For most of us, our basic sense of belonging and security comes from being part of a family, the group that satisfies our primary emotional needs. Its size can vary from culture to culture, ranging from the nuclear family of many Western societies to the large extended family characteristic of many other cultures. For some children it can mean no more than their mother, a single parent, living in a city far from any kin. For others it can mean the grandparents, uncle, aunt, and cousins who actually live in the same house, as well as other relatives who live in the same town or in other parts of the country, all being regarded as real and important members of one extended family.

Whatever their cultural background or size, most families value contact with their kin. The benefits of this contact are obvious to anyone who has ever seen children enjoying one another's company at a family gathering. But, in addition, being part of such a gathering gives children a real sense of their wider identity, of how they fit into a network of people who value them, and in which they play a small but important part.

Teaching children about family history can also help to strengthen their sense of identity, of being a link in a chain that goes back many generations, and will probably continue for many generations to come. When children reach the later primary-school years, they usually become interested in finding out about the lives of their grand-parents, great-grandparents, and other relatives. As a result, they see themselves as part of a wider family group which not only has many living members, but which also stretches back into the past. This can give children a comforting sense of security and belonging, and adds a further dimension to their self-concept.

So, look after old family photographs, letters, and other documents. Bringing them out on a wintry evening to look at them in front of the fire can provide hours of happy reminiscing, help to forge a strong sense of family identity, and give your child a broader concept of who they are.

Take for example, the young girl who had discovered a box of family photographs in an old trunk in the base-ment, and was looking through them on the living-room floor.

'Who's this, Mum?' she asked, holding up an old sepia studio portrait of a bearded man in a top hat and his wife in long dress and bonnet.

'They, my dear, are your great-great-grandparents.'

'Your great-grandparents, Mum?'

'That's right. They were among the first settlers in this

area, towards the end of the nineteenth century. Your great-great-grandfather cleared a large area of land for a farm, then started a grocery business. By the early 1890s he owned the first real department store in the city.'

'And his wife?'

'She managed to raise eight children, helped to break in the farm, then supported your great-great-grandfather in developing his business. In her later life she worked hard to improve facilities at the local schools, because she was a great believer in education for women.'

'How come you know all this, Mum?'

'Because I'm interested in finding out about our family. It somehow gives me a sense of belonging. I guess I also feel proud of what members of our family have achieved. I think, well, if they could do that, maybe I can, too.'

Her daughter was thoughtful. 'I know what you mean, Mum. I'm glad I found this photo. Do you think we could have it framed and hang it in the house somewhere? It'll make our family feel a bit bigger!'

'Sure. What a good idea!'

Other Groups

There are many other organizations children can belong to that give them a sense of identity, such as a school, sports team, youth group, or church. Not only can children feel a sense of pride just from belonging to such groups, but their self-esteem can be boosted as they master the new skills which the group teaches and expects them to perform.

In teams of various sorts there can be the extra satisfaction of knowing that when the team is successful, you have played a part in achieving that success. This kind of satisfaction has a special quality to it because it combines the pleasure of doing a job well with a sense of comradeship and belonging.

Young people can rediscover their culture with pleasure and pride.

Cultural Identity

Belonging to a culture with a unique character deriving from its own history, folklore, and customs can be an important part of a person's identity. Its customs can provide ways of understanding and dealing with the major milestones in human life, such as birth, marriage, and death. Learning about and identifying with their culture can have a very positive effect on a young person's self-confidence, and their sense of having a place in the world.

Some young people are members of a minority cultural or ethnic group, either because their families have emigrated from their homeland or their culture has been swamped by colonization. They should be given the opportunity to discover their roots and to learn the values and customs of their parents or grandparents. It may be that because they want to identify with the dominant culture as they grow up, they won't show much interest as children in learning about their heritage. But as young adults they may rediscover it with pleasure and pride.

Gangs

An interesting example of the power of the group, and of our need to belong, is the allegiance which some young men have to semi-outlaw groups such as motor-bike gangs. Most members have a strong sense of loyalty to their gang not just because they are all good mates together, but because the gang offers some major psychological benefits.

Firstly, there is the simple comfort of belonging. For some young men, coming from childhoods of neglect and deprivation, a gang may provide their first experiences of belonging to a group where they are liked, appreciated, and respected. Gangs also give their members a very strong sense of identity by dramatically highlighting the differences between themselves and 'straight' society in the way they dress and behave. Also, because they present an image of menace and potential violence which can intimidate other people, gang members experience a sense of power, of being larger than life.

In order to join a gang, prospective members must go through initiation rites or behave in ways that show they have what it takes to be accepted. Passing the entry requirements gives a sense of accomplishment. Then, as a member, there is further pride and peer recognition to be experienced in living up to the gang's code of conduct. Finally, the gang gives a very strong sense of comradeship and support.

Put all these ingredients together and what do you get? A very potent tonic for self-esteem. As one bikie expressed it: 'You feel something. You feel good to belong in a group like that.' Many other groups offer the same kinds of psychological rewards as a gang — belonging, identity, accomplishment, power, pride, and support — with just as much potential for enhancing self-esteem, but with much less likelihood of being arrested!

Religion

Religions provide a system for understanding the nature of the universe and our place in it. For believers a religion can give a sense of meaning, dignity, and personal worth, which are all important aspects of self-esteem.

If you want your children to be active members of the religious group you belong to, and to remain in it as adults, try not to force them to take part in it. Discuss the issue together, encourage their involvement, and by your own behaviour provide a positive example of the benefits of your religion. If membership of a religion is to mean anything to us as adults, it will be on the basis of free and informed choice leading to willing commitment. Giving children no choice about taking part in religious activities can cause rebellious refusal to be involved as they become older, or lead to unthinking participation out of sheer habit, which is unlikely to be of any benefit to them.

My own feeling is that we should respect the judgement and intelligence of our children by telling them about our own religious beliefs if we have any, explaining why we hold them, and inviting them to take part if they want.

Whether or not we belong to a particular religion, we owe it to our children to answer as best we can their questions about the spiritual aspects of life, and the 'big' issues of meaning and purpose which we all have to come to terms with in some way.

We can explain that over the course of human history many different answers have been given to these big questions, leading people to express their spirituality in different ways. We can tell them what we know about the major religions of the world, and encourage them to find out more for themselves so that they can eventually make a free choice about how they will respond to the spiritual dimension of life. Even if you are a born-again atheist, allow your children the intellectual freedom to discover their own answers as you discovered yours.

The Planet

Belonging to a national or racial group can enhance our feeling of pride and self-worth, but the sad fact is that conflict between nations and ethnic groups has been the cause of immeasurable suffering to our species. Fortunately, the rapid development of transport and communication technology over the last generation is leading to a noticeable change in our perspective. We can now see clearly and immediately on live colour television the global impact of political decisions, economic policies, wars, natural disasters, and pollution. It's now obvious that the well-being and destiny of all the nations on this planet are linked. We are all passengers on a tiny spaceship called Earth, dependent on one another for our ultimate survival.

The time is right to encourage our young people to identify not just with their country or culture, but with the future of their planet. They are already well aware of the dangers of global pollution. It would be good if they could derive a sense of identity and self-worth from their commitment to the survival and future of the only home we've got.

In Summary

The effects on self-esteem of belonging to groups of different sizes and kinds can be very powerful. Family, school, church, and sporting and cultural groups all have the potential to give children a sense of identity, worth, and purpose.

What happens in families probably has the greatest effect on children's basic self-esteem, but membership of other groups can develop important aspects of how children see themselves. It can help them to appreciate who they are, what they can do well, their place in the world, and the important contribution they can make to the goals of a group. There is a special satisfaction in being able to see past our individual wishes and needs to contribute to the success of a team or organization with which we identify.

8

School

The two institutions in Western culture which have the most powerful effect in shaping children's self-esteem are family and school. Of the two, the family is the more fundamental and potent force, but school can run a very close second, particularly as children grow older.

Schooling and Society

Society has decided that the benefits of formal education are so important that schooling should be compulsory. We now expect children to be in school for about six hours a day, five days a week, from about the age of five years until at least fifteen or sixteen years, and parents can be prosecuted if they don't make sure that their children attend regularly. Today, attending school is childhood's central task in most Western countries. School takes priority for children just as work takes priority for adults, with family and leisure activities fitted in around them.

There is now also an increasing expectation that children will spend more time in formal education at each end of the age spectrum, starting earlier at preschool and staying on longer at high school after the minimum leaving age. Governments pride themselves on figures showing that greater percentages of young people are staying on at school longer, then carrying on to tertiary education programmes, because extended education is seen to be linked with a country's prosperity.

Many parents put a lot of thought, time, and money into ensuring that their children's education is as success-ful as it can be. We want our children to do well at school because we can see, from our perspective, how important educational qualifications are for their future. But because of the value society places on education, and because of our hopes as parents, children can be placed under great pressure to succeed.

Furthermore, major aspects of the schooling system are perfectly designed to highlight some children's weak-nesses, exposing them frequently to painful feelings of failure or inadequacy. This, of course, can have seriously negative effects on their self-esteem. These aspects include schools' primary focus and emphasis on academic tasks, an assessment system which is based on externally imposed grades and implies comparison with other students, and enforced peer contact, which some children find difficult to cope with.

Academic Tasks

The daily business of schooling is carried out for the most part through language in its spoken and written forms. Children acquire knowledge in classrooms from oral in-struction, discussion, and the printed word; only a very small percentage of the learning that takes place in schools is through direct experience. In fact, schools are largely segregated from the wider life of our society. They bring the world into the classroom in symbolic form, through the spoken word, written text, pictures, and diagrams. In school, children learn mostly by talking, reading, and writing about life, rather than experiencing it.

Whether or not this is a good thing, the inescapable fact is that not all children are equally able to carry out the major expectation which school places upon them: to manipulate abstract symbols skilfully. By this I mean the ability to discuss, read, write, and calculate. These are the essential, prerequisite skills for carrying out the academic tasks which take up most of the school day, but which not all children have the ability to perform equally well.

Children all have natural aptitudes for some tasks, which are learnt easily and quickly, while other tasks take a lot of practice and repetition, sometimes for little apparent gain. Think of your own experience. There are some things which you know you are not very good at, in spite of trying hard, and others that you seem to have a talent for and do quite well, with little or no formal training.

The same situation applies to children. Some show early evidence of ability in construction-type activities, some have excellent physical co-ordination, and some learn to speak early. With regard to academic skills, some children learn to read and write more quickly and easily than their peers. The majority of children who are provided with competent teaching, time to practise, and encouragement, will learn at an average rate. But some, unfortunately, will not.

Some children are born with below-average general intellectual ability, which limits their capacity to understand and carry out academic tasks. Some have at least average intellectual skills but, because of a specific learning disability, struggle for most of their school-days to achieve even average levels in reading and spelling. Some children have subtle language disorders which make it difficult for them to express their thoughts clearly, and others may suffer from a degree of hyperactivity (attention deficit disorder), which makes sitting still and attending almost impossible. For these children, school can become a very punishing place. They are constantly confronted with their inability to do what comes so naturally to their class-mates, and this is understandably very harmful to their self-image and confidence.

The case of learning disabled youngsters is particularly poignant because, despite good understanding and oral language skills, they are often unable to read at an age-appropriate level and may have great difficulty with writing. They therefore tend to avoid these tasks after being at school for a few years, and may be considered lazy by their teachers because they seem to be bright, but the standard of their academic work doesn't match up to their apparent promise. Such youngsters eventually tend to label themselves as 'dumb', and the whole schooling process can become very frustrating and stressful for them.

To try to understand the situation of children who struggle to succeed at academic tasks, imagine what it would be like to have a job where you found it very difficult to master what you were expected to do, where your workmates seemed to have no problem in coping, and where you were constantly singled out for extra assistance, coaching, and criticism by your employer. Imagine doing this kind of job day after day for ten years, and not being allowed to quit. What would your self-esteem be like at the end of it?

I remember one young boy who had difficulty from his earliest days at school. As a preschooler, Simon had been very active, and at kindergarten had much preferred being outdoors on the slide and in the sandpit to being involved with indoor activities, such as painting and puzzles.

When Simon reached school age, his progress with reading and writing was very slow. His handwriting was big and clumsy, he often reversed his letters, and he had major problems with learning to spell. In reading, the words he learnt one day were forgotten the next, and he seemed to have trouble with even the little, high-frequency words such as 'the', 'for', and 'was'. On the other hand, his oral language skills were good, and he was quick to pick up new concepts in maths.

By the end of Simon's second year at school, despite extra lessons and individual support with his reading and writing, both at home and school, the gap between him and his class-mates was widening. He was becoming discouraged about his progress, saying things like 'I'll never learn to read' and 'I'm just dumb'.

An assessment by the school psychologist showed that Simon's verbal intelligence was, in fact, above average. The picture was becoming clearer that Simon had a specific learning disability. In other words, in spite of normal intelligence he had an innate difficulty in coping with the processes of reading and writing. This meant not only that Simon would probably continue to need specialist support for most of his schooling, but also that his teachers would have to show great patience, understanding, and flexibility in helping him to achieve his academic potential.

For the sake of Simon's self-esteem, it was clearly very important for his parents firstly to accept that he had a genuine disability, although an invisible one. They would need to understand that even simple academic tasks would require much greater effort and concentration for Simon to complete than most other children of his age. Finally, they would need to be actively on the look-out to identify and nurture any strengths and talents Simon might have. This would help bolster his sagging self-esteem, and compensate for the damage being done to his self-image by his failures with schoolwork.

Assessment

Assessment of progress has always been an important part of formal education, and it clearly serves a useful purpose. Teachers, in fact, have a responsibility to check on whether pupils have learnt the skills which are the goals of a unit of work. But an unfortunate side-effect of the assessment process is the inevitable comparison students make among themselves about their performance. Regular assessment of skills and progress means that young people receive frequent messages about whether they are succeeding in the system, and how their performance compares with that of their peers. Students compare marks or grades, and take them as an evaluation not just of their performance in an isolated area of skills or knowledge, but of their total functioning as a person. Their *overall* self-concept is affected accordingly.

For those who are achieving at an average level, or above, in their reading, maths, English, and so on, it is unlikely there will be a problem. But for those young people who are not succeeding academically, school can become a place where you go to have your self-esteem battered on a daily basis.

Peers

School is also a place of compulsory, enforced contact with peers. Children have almost no choice about whether they go to school, or whether they will take part in the day's range of activities. They are expected to be at school, to do what the teacher asks, and also to interact with their peers. Much of what happens at school is done in groups, and children are expected to be part of those groups.

In some ways, what happens at a social level among children is the most real and vital part of school life for them. The social undercurrents of classroom life are remembered long after the academic content of lessons is forgotten. Some of this interaction is positive, leading to the formation of individual friendships and closeness between groups of children with similar interests, 'gangs' in the best sense. But not for all children. There are always one or two in any class who lack the social skills to be included in any group, and they suffer because of it.

Children often fall out with one another, then make friends with someone else or get back together, but some children find it hard to make any friends at all. They may hang around on the fringes of games and often tend to play with younger children. In extreme cases they may not just be isolated or rejected by their age-mates, but be bullied or victimized as well.

Friendships become increasingly important as children move through primary into secondary school, and the feeling of being socially rejected and isolated can be very painful. A major part of the self-image of older children is their social acceptability, and young people who feel they have no friends devalue themselves because of it. In the most extreme cases, young people who attempt suicide often feel that they have been rejected by their peers, and usually come from a family background of tension and unhappiness as well.

What Can Schools Do?

Despite the comments in the previous paragraphs, it is a fact that most children enjoy and benefit from their time at school. All children will have some bad experiences in the areas of learning, assessment, or peer relationships during their school years, but on balance the scales tip definitely towards the positive side for the great majority of students. Educators nevertheless accept that they have a responsibility to minimize the potentially harmful effects of some major aspects of the schooling process, and try their best to do so, but there is still more that could be done.

Given that all children have different profiles of talents and strengths, and not all are capable of average performance in the area of academic skills, it would be very beneficial for some children if as much emphasis and importance could be given to non-academic aspects of the curriculum as to the three Rs.

Today's schools originated as a system for teaching literacy and numeracy, and this is still their major focus at the primary level. Even though the range of subjects now widens considerably as children progress from junior to senior levels, the daily business of schools is still fundamentally academic. Most of what happens in classrooms, at all levels of the education system, is based on the abstract symbols of language in spoken and written forms. But the ability to deal with abstract symbols does not come naturally and easily to all children. Their talents may lie in other areas.

You need only look at any student report form to see the priority that schools give to academic performance in relation to other skills. The core academic subjects of reading, language, and maths at the primary level, and English, maths, social studies, and science at the secondary level, take precedence. These subjects head the ranking order, with music, art, technical subjects, and physical education bringing up the rear.

While this order may reflect what school has traditionally been all about, it does not reflect the ability profile of a significant number of students, and, in fact, devalues their talents. Schools usually make some effort to acknowledge skills in non-academic areas but the greatest weight and emphasis is placed on academic success.

It would be possible for schools to have a conscious and deliberate policy of genuine acknowledgement for achievement in all areas of school life, which would provide recognition of the individual talents of all children. Primary schools are usually quite good at doing this, with a system of presenting awards at assemblies for a wide range of successes and special efforts, often in non-curriculum areas.

It has, of course, been part of educational philosophy for a long time that teachers should, wherever possible, highlight a child's strengths, rather than focus on failings, but the emphasis on academic skills makes it difficult to do that for some children. Ideally, the focus in classrooms should be on what children *can* do rather than on what they *can't* do. A simple method to encourage this is for students to keep an 'I can ... ' list of their achievements, which they add to as they learn new skills, and an 'I'm good at ...' list to remind them of their strengths. But if children are to feel that everyone's talents are genuinely regarded as important, this needs to be an explicit and actively encouraged part of a school's teaching philosophy.

Self-assessment and Independence in Learning

The assessment of skills and progress is an integral part of schooling. Children's schoolwork is continually being evaluated and graded by teachers according to standards of accuracy, competence, effort, and presentation. In principle, there is nothing wrong with this, of course, because assessment is a necessary part of the teaching process.

My concern, however, is that when children are constantly judged according to external standards of acceptable performance, they lose the ability to evaluate their work for themselves and the belief that their own self-evaluations are valid and important. It can be a subtle, insidiously destructive process as children's capacity to reflect on and make judgements about their own performance is gradually eroded because they are very seldom given the chance to do so.

Schools are well-meaning organizations, but they are also basically regimented and restrictive. They limit children's opportunities to make significant choices about what, how, or when they will learn. Although most schools claim to encourage the development of independence in learning, the way they are organized encourages the exact opposite. Schools and teachers make most decisions for children about how their day will be organized, what they will learn, and even how their work should be set out on the page. Pupils have almost no input into how schools are run, except sometimes through student councils, which are often powerless, or as a token representative on the school board. Subject choice is almost non-existent until secondary school, and even then almost always from a traditionally academic range. Teachers' assessments of performance are usually one-sided, final, and absolute.

The end result of a minium of ten years of this kind of day-to-day experience for young people can be a loss of their natural initiative, a reliance on others for decision-making and goal-setting, and a loss of the ability to evaluate their own behaviour in terms of their own perceived values. The development of a strong sense of self-worth, competence, and self-trust is the result of many opportunities to make choices, see them through, then evaluate the results in order to have a guide for future choices. Doing this hundreds of times on small matters over many years helps children to become self-reliant and develop confidence in their own judgement.

Schools can encourage the growth of self-reliance and independence in their students by giving them an effective say in some aspects of running the school, greater input into the structure of their own learning programmes, and, especially, by involving them in the assessment of their own work and behaviour.

I have seen a classroom of ten- to twelve-year-old students who were following completely individual study programmes within the usual subject structure, making their own choices about when they would work on particular topics so long as they were completed by a certain date. The children responded enthusiastically to this system and it's not hard to see why. They were being given choices about how to organize their day and week.

Being given a choice implies trust. Making a choice means having to think about options and evaluate them. And because self-assessment was part of the process, the children had to think critically about their own standards, strengths, and weaknesses. This system engaged the children, made them active partners in their education, and helped them to become independent, self-directed learners. Benefits for their self-esteem would be inevitable.

Individual learning programmes are a long way from what happens in most classrooms, but many primary teachers include aspects of this approach in their teaching practice. One crucial element which all teachers can easily use is to encourage students to evaluate at least some of their own work. Pupils can assess their performance in terms of effort, presentation, and overall worth, or comment on how well they feel they have achieved the objectives for the unit of work. Their assessments could supplement or even sometimes replace the teacher's grades.

Apart from this more formal kind of evaluation, there are scores of opportunities every day for teachers to ask children for their opinion of the work they have just done, what they particularly like about it, and what could perhaps be improved on. Older children can enjoy and benefit from an individual conference once a term to talk about how they feel things are going, areas where they are doing well, and subjects where they need a bit of help or need to put in a greater effort. It is reasonably easy to make self-assessment a natural and valued part of everyday classroom life. Its benefits for students include more accurate self-perception, a greater sense of responsibility, and enhanced self-respect.

Individual learning programmes are not 'pie in the sky'. Many primary teachers now use the 'learning centre' system of activities set up around the classroom for pupils to work on when they have finished assigned tasks. Children need to be introduced gradually to the process of working independently, and the learning-centre system is certainly a big step in the right direction. Even if some teachers may be sceptical about the feasibility of individualized learning, the increasing availability of computers in classrooms will eventually make it an every-day reality.

Self-esteem Programmes

Many schools today are including components in their health studies programmes which are specifically aimed at improving children's self-esteem. Recent years have also seen a proliferation of drug education programmes, almost all of which focus on enhancing self-esteem as the major factor in preventing young people from becoming involved in drug use. The topics covered in these health-based pro-grammes usually include communication skills, assertive-ness, decision-making, peer pressure, and helping children to understand more about their bodies, their feelings, and the good things about themselves as individuals.

While this focus on self-esteem is commendable, there is not much evidence yet to show that such programmes are effective. The major problem is that the issues are dealt with in the artificial environment of the classroom, which reduces the chances that the skills and attitudes they teach will transfer to real-life situations. To give the programmes the best chance of success, schools need to reinforce them by making sure that their messages are part of everyday teaching practice. When effective communication, assert-iveness, problem-solving, and respect for ourselves and others are part of the total school programme, then children have an opportunity to learn and use these skills in their daily lives.

If Your Child Needs Help

If your child has learning difficulties, finds it hard to relate to other children, or has trouble adjusting to the demands and expectations of classroom life, then school can become an unpleasant place for them, a place they would rather avoid.

If you feel that your child's self-esteem is being damaged by their school experiences, then don't delay in seeking help. Arrange a meeting with the class teacher to discuss your concerns, and if this doesn't seem to produce an improvement, ask to see a senior teacher or the principal. Schools can usually provide resources and programmes for pupils who need extra support, and can call on specialist services for assessment and advice if necessary. In most cases it is possible, through co-ordinated planning and effort, to help children who have special educational or behavioural needs.

In Summary

Although not as influential as the family, schools certainly have the power to affect children's self-esteem, for good or ill. Some major aspects of the schooling process, such as its emphasis on academic skills, can highlight a child's lack of ability in certain areas and make them feel inadequate. Because educational success is so highly valued in our society, children who perform at a below-average level in school can feel devalued as individuals. Schools can help by:

- Recognizing and valuing children's achievements in non-academic areas;
- Giving students the opportunity for a real say and input in the life of the classroom and school;
- Making self-assessment part of daily teaching practice;
- Ensuring that the components of health-based self-esteem programmes are instituted and supported across the total life of the school;
- Actively seeking opportunities to increase children's self-reliance, independence, and responsibility for their own learning.

In my experience, schools generally work hard at making education a stimulating, positive, and satisfying experience for their students. In most educational facilities, from kindergarten to college, the dedication and professionalism of staff, and their commitment to the well-being of students, are outstanding. All that needs to be added is the protection and enhancement of children's self-esteem as a conscious and valued part of a school's philosophy.

9

Gender

It's likely that the very first words spoken about us at the moment of our birth were to tell our parents whether they had a son or a daughter. From the instant we're born, gender is a major aspect of our identity. In this chapter we look at the relationship between sex roles and self-concept, in particular at how our differing expectations for male and female children can limit their chances to develop their individual talents.

Gender Differences in Behaviour

Across generations and societies, there have been obvious differences in the behaviour of men and women. Some tasks, functions, and attitudes are usually associated with women, and others with men, to the extent that we talk about *sex roles*: a set of behaviours or tasks which are usually performed by one sex or the other. While these behavioural differences may have originated from the physical differences between males and females, a crucial question in today's society is: 'How much of the difference between male and female behaviour is learned, and how much is due to biology, to our genetic inheritance?'

Because of the influence of feminism, we have become very aware that some of our beliefs about how men and women behave are based on custom, assumption, and prejudice, rather than on biological fact. In many areas we have had to re-examine and rethink our expectations about what women and men can do, and we are now much more careful not to force girls and boys, women and men, to conform to stereotypes of how we think they should behave.

We need to know as accurately as we can how much of gender-related behaviour is influenced by heredity and how much is shaped through custom and teaching. This knowledge will not only have an effect on what young people are encouraged to strive for and achieve in their lives, but it will also help determine what they can accept and feel pride about in their femininity or masculinity.

Social Influence

No one has been able to pick up any significant differences in the behaviour of newborn girls and boys, but as they grow older, behavioural differences between the sexes become increasingly apparent. What causes most girls and boys to behave in ways that are seen as typical of their sex? Do parents and other adults encourage and teach them to behave according to expectations of how they *should* behave? Do we mould their behaviour to match the social stereotype?

In recent years a lot of emphasis has been placed on highlighting the social influences which can shape children's behaviour. According to this approach, children learn to be typical boys or typical girls.

In one research study, an observer recorded the way adults spoke to and played with a little girl in a park. The girl was then dressed as a boy, and the comments and behaviour of adults changed accordingly. In other words, the same child was treated differently by grown-ups according to their perception of her gender. The significance of this study is that it dramatically emphasizes the effect of social learning. It is just one trivial episode, one tiny fragment in a child's life, but imagine the accumulated effect of years of similar experiences on the way a child perceives herself or himself.

There is no doubt that social influences can be very powerful. Some are subtle, some blatant. Children can be actively encouraged to behave in girlish or boyish ways by saying things like 'Girls don't play rough games' or 'Boys shouldn't cry'. And then there is the praise for conforming: 'She's such a little lady!' or 'He's a real boy!'

But social influences are not the whole story. Over recent years many parents have taken the messages of feminism to heart, and have tried to bring up their children in a gender-neutral way. These parents have dutifully tried to avoid sex-typing their children, particularly in the area of play. And how successful have they been? Not very, it seems, according to comments I have heard, and observations with our own children. Boys and girls show strong preferences for certain kinds of play, and are very resistant to switching brands. If encouraged, girls will play a little with trucks and space-ships, and boys with dolls, but for most children their real energy, persistence, and concentration seem to be reserved for the games which form part of their sex-role stereotype.

What Does Research Say?

Research in developmental psychology confirms significant differences between the sexes, some of which seem to be biologically based. For example, girls learn to talk sooner than boys, and boys are much more likely to develop speech and language problems. Girls are quicker to toilet train. Boys are much more likely to be behaviour problems at school, to have difficulty learning to read, and to be diagnosed as learning disabled. From an early age, girls show more sympathy to children in distress, and are more nurturing to younger children. Some researchers have reported the possibility of structural differences between the brains of males and females, which could be related to the skills at which boys and girls excel: verbal for girls, and mathematical–spatial for boys.

Other similar examples of gender differences in behaviour are hard to explain on the basis of social learning alone. After all, many other species on the planet have clear, in-born differences in behaviour between females and males — why should humans be the exception? And I've often wondered how parents could be so successful in effort-lessly teaching sex-role behaviour, almost without being aware of it, when all our other efforts to shape up the little devils are such hard work, to so little effect!

Children Are Individuals

So the answer to our earlier question seems to be that both heredity and learning play a part in explaining how girls and boys behave the way they do. Some aspects of their behaviour seem to be 'wired in' along the lines of tradi-tional ideas about the things that girls and boys tend to do, while other aspects are the result of social condition-ing and prejudice. But how do we know which is which?

The best answer to this question lies in a point I have made before: know, and respect, your child's individual-ity. If we want to give our children the chance to be what-ever they are capable of, we should look hard to discover the pattern of talents and abilities they are born with. We should try not to look at them through the pink- or blue-tinted spectacles of gender stereotypes.

Give your child opportunities to take part in a wide range of activities, and watch the responses carefully. If your daughter shows talent in kicking a ball, give her the option of playing soccer. If your son shows an interest in dance, enrol him in a local dance class. Don't close doors

*If your daughter shows talent in kicking a ball,
give her the option of playing soccer.*

to your child on the basis of sex-role prejudice. If your
teenage daughter decides she would like to become a
truck-driver, don't stand in her way! The chance to fulfil
our potential, and display excellence in an area of natural
aptitude, brings the possibility of great satisfaction and a
powerful boost to our self-esteem.

Take, for example, eleven-year-old Laura. No doubt about
it, she was a tomboy. She loved to be outdoors riding her
bike, climbing trees, and playing football with her three

older brothers. She could throw a ball hard and straight. And she hated to wear skirts or dresses. For all these reasons, Laura and her mother were often in conflict.

Before Laura was born her mother prayed that she might at last have a daughter, a lovely little girl who would be dainty, delicate, and feminine — a girl who could be dressed in ribbons and lace; a girl who wouldn't be loud, boisterous, and always grubby like her three sons. And what did she get? Laura!

'Why won't you wear a dress to school, Laura?' was the way weekday mornings usually began.

'Because I don't like them, Mum. I hate dresses. You can't do anything in them. And besides, they look dumb. I want to wear jeans.'

'Just once, dear. Please wear a dress for me. Or a skirt. You look so lovely in that green skirt ... '

'No, Mum, I'm wearing these jeans. See you after school. Bye.'

It was hard for Laura's mother as she watched her daughter play rough and tumble games, ignore the birthday gifts of dolls and toy ponies in her bedroom, and come home from school with scratched elbows and a dirty face. It was hard to go along on Saturdays to watch her play soccer with boys, even though Laura was good at it and was a valued team member.

But eventually, with difficulty, Laura's mother came to accept that this was the way her daughter was, and nothing was going to change that. She came to accept that she would have to let go her dreams of a dainty and feminine daughter, and value Laura for her own unique strengths and talents. When that finally happened, Laura was able to relax, be herself, and begin to feel good about who she was.

The education system has in the past played a major role in limiting opportunities and options for both sexes. In ways both subtle and sledge-hammer obvious, educational customs reinforced sex-role stereotypes. They effectively prevented girls and boys from making subject choices that challenged gender taboos. In educational texts from primers to college, illustrations, photographs, and the use of sexist language have unthinkingly reinforced traditional male and female roles and career-choice stereotypes. Fortunately, these customs and practices are now being actively questioned and changed. For example, it is good to go into schools today and see girls taking metalwork, and boys taking home economics.

There is also increasing awareness of how boys can dominate classroom activities and a teacher's attention, depriving some girls of learning opportunities, and reinforcing their traditional image as unassertive spectators. Although there is still a long way to go on this issue, girls and boys are now at least getting a chance to take part in a wider range of learning experiences, and to make career choices that suit them as individuals, regardless of their sex.

Although it is easy to see how girls have been disadvantaged by the education system, and parents are now more watchful not to limit their daughters' potential by reinforcing sex-role stereotypes, the same caution applies to boys. Just as girls must be able to be assertive when they need to be, or pursue a career in, say, engineering, boys should be able to feel comfortable about expressing their feelings, or working in a daycare centre, if that's what they want to do.

Sexual Identity

One final point needs to be made about the relationship between gender and self-esteem. When children reach puberty, their stirring sexuality can mean having to painfully restructure their self-image, and for a small number of teenagers this can be particularly difficult. Most of us develop feelings of attraction for members of the opposite sex, but this is not always the case. A small percentage of young people, through no choice or wish of their own, find themselves physically attracted towards others of the same sex. Coping with sexual feelings and behaviour is hard enough for teenagers without the added anxiety and stress of realizing that they want to express their sexuality in a way that many people disapprove of.

The crucial issue for these young people, however, is their parents' attitude. If they feel that their parents are uncomfortable with, or even hostile to, the possibility of their being lesbian or gay, and that they cannot talk about it with them, it makes it very much harder for them to work through the issue. In these circumstances there is enormous potential for damage to their sense of self-worth, even to the extent of considering suicide. As Felix Donnelly writes in *Teenage Sexuality* (GP Books, 1989):

> ... the issue of sexual identity is not just about whether the young person wonders whether they are gay or lesbian, but is wider in the sense that whatever their sexual attraction might be (heterosexual or homosexual), young people wonder how they will be able to function in that role and whether they will be acceptable to others.... Young people can agonise secretly over these sexual issues even to the point of despair.
>
> It has been my experience over many years in dealing with young people who have attempted suicide that sexual identity in its broadest sense has frequently been a significant factor in their despair....
>
> It is important for anyone who believes themselves to be homosexual to talk and think it through carefully, then accept whatever the reality might be. What one does with one's sexuality after that point is another matter. What parents need to understand and help with is this initial acceptance of a reality.

Feeling comfortable with their sexuality and sexual identity is a crucial developmental task for all teenagers, and its outcome will have major impact on their sense of self-worth. Our role as parents is to make our own standards and values clear while being as open as we can to discussion. If either you or your teenager should find it hard to talk about sex, or if she or he seems to be going through a particularly difficult time, don't hesitate to seek professional counselling through their school or a helping agency. If in doubt, your family doctor will be able to advise you about local resources.

In Summary

Our gender is a fundamental part of our identity, not so much because of our physical equipment but because of the traditional roles and behaviours associated with our sex. While sex roles may have originated along with our physical evolution, they have also been shaped by culture and custom.

We can guard against the danger of turning our children into replicas of gender stereotypes if we make it our business to know and understand them as individuals. Once we have done that we can help them to accept their personal profile of talents and abilities, challenge the barriers of sexism when they need to, and work towards the goal of fulfilling their unique potential. If they achieve that, a healthy self-concept is just about guaranteed.

10

Praise

Think back to the last time you were praised. How did it make you feel? If the praise was genuine, it probably made you feel good all over, as a person. We take the effect of praise for granted, but it's amazing how just a few words of recognition for achievement or effort can have such an influence on our perception of ourselves, and our sense of well-being.

There can be no doubt that praise is food for our self-esteem. It is hard to imagine how anyone could develop a sense of self-worth without receiving some recognition and affirmation of their achievements and strengths. And yet, although we all recognize the power of praise and its importance for our psychological health, it can be a scarce commodity in some homes, not to mention the wider community. Think again. When was the last time you praised your child? Today? Last week? No doubt you've seen the bumper sticker 'Have you hugged your kid today?' Regular doses of genuine, realistic praise are just about as important.

Self-concept

Children need praise to:

- Feel good about themselves;
- Motivate and encourage them during new learning;
- Help them to develop a sense of competence; and
- Become aware of their strengths as part of their overall self-concept.

As they attempt new tasks and develop new skills, children need feedback from the adults around them about how well they are doing. Whether it's learning to swim, ride a bike, read, or draw, recognition of effort and improvement helps to motivate them when the going gets a little tough, and to feel good about themselves as a result. Each new success gradually builds up a feeling of confidence, and a perception of themselves as being capable and competent. Praise provides the psychological fuel to keep the whole process moving along.

If your child has an area of special ability or talent, acknowledge it. This can encourage them to develop it through perseverance and practice, and to accept it as a part of their self-concept.

Some parents may feel a little uncomfortable about this idea, but there is nothing wrong with acknowledging ability. We need to be aware of both our relative weaknesses and strengths to develop a realistic perception of ourselves as individuals, and an accurate self-perception is the starting point for a successful adjustment to life.

How to Praise

The first rule is simply to do it! As I implied earlier, it's a sad fact that praise can sometimes appear to be in danger of disappearing in our society, because it is heard so rarely. Hard work, skill, and helpful service often go unacknowledged and apparently unnoticed. There may be some slight excuse for this in the wider community because we expect people to do their work for pay, not praise and thanks, but we shouldn't really operate like that in the family. If we do, it will be at a cost to the self-concept of our children.

'I' Statements

To be effective, praise needs to be genuine. Insincere, empty praise or unrealistic compliments are at best a waste of time and at worst can be counter-productive. An automatic, unfeeling 'That's nice, dear' can send the disappointing and frustrating message to our children that we're not really interested in their achievements. Also, if children feel that you don't really mean it when you praise them, they can interpret your words as an attempt to make them feel better over something that they are not sure they have done well. These kinds of messages are more likely to undermine their confidence than build it up.

To avoid apparent insincerity try using an 'I' statement, such as, 'I think you did a really good job on that school project' or ' I liked the way you shared your toys when Jamie came to play today'. When you begin your comment with 'I' you are more likely to convey the genuine feeling that should underlie any praise. And just as with effective listening, eye contact can help, too.

A much more subtle but equally important reason for using 'I' statements is that they make it clear that you are expressing your own personal opinion and feeling about your child's behaviour, according to your own values. When we say things like 'That's excellent' or 'You did very well' or 'Your behaviour was dreadful', it can sound as though we are evaluating our children against some absolute standard of good or bad, pass or fail. It may seem like a very fine distinction to make, but there is a real difference between the two types of statement. An expression of genuine, personal feeling is more likely to touch our children and encourage them to reflect on what they have done than an impersonal judgement, even if that judgement is positive.

The purpose of praise is not to make children want to conform to certain standards for the reward of our approval, but to help them to be aware of and think about their strengths and the things they do well. In the end, they should be able to pat themselves on the back for their own accomplishments according to their own values, and not be dependent on the judgement of others. They should be able to say to themselves, 'I think I did a good job there' or 'I'm pleased with the way I did that', and be satisfied with their own judgement. We can guide them in that direction not just by the way we express our praise but also by including a question to encourage self-evaluation. For example: 'I thought you played with a lot more confidence in the second half today. How did you feel about it?' or 'I was impressed with the effort you put into your project. Were you pleased with it?' In this way we can help children to think about, evaluate, and control their own behaviour.

Be Specific

Praise is more effective if it is specific. The comment, 'I like the way you've used different colours and black outlines in your drawing', is much more likely to guide, encourage, and motivate a young artist than 'That's a nice picture'. Also, to be specific we have to think a little about what we are going to say, which is a safeguard against automatic, empty, or unrealistic praise. But the bottom line is that just about any praise is better than none. There will obviously be times when a brief but sincere 'Well done!' is what's called for and will do the job just fine.

Thanks

Thanks can be a form of praise, too. When we say something like 'I really appreciated the way you helped out with the gardening today', we are saying more than just 'Thank you'. We are, in fact, recognizing a range of positive qualities, including effort, co-operation, and almost certainly some self-sacrifice as well! It's not a bad policy to look for one thing every day that we can praise our children for, and included in that should be reasons to say 'Thanks':

- 'Thanks for tidying your room today without my having to nag you.'
- 'Thanks for being patient with your little brother this morning — I know he was being a real pain.'
- 'Thanks for phoning when you knew you were going to be late last night — we really worry when you're not home on time.'

If we don't acknowledge such features as effort, consideration, and patience, we shouldn't be surprised if they don't occur as often as we would like.

Look for the Positive

In the day-to-day business of being a parent it's easy to fall into the trap of focusing on the negative, and to comment only when things haven't been done, or haven't been done right. We sometimes need to make a conscious effort to look for the good things that our children are doing, and acknowledge them. In my experience, there is a noticeable and very pleasant quality in the working atmosphere of classrooms where teachers make a point of noticing and commenting on achievement and effort. The children seem happier, more energetic, and more co-operative because they feel good about themselves.

It was always a pleasure for me to visit Ms Patterson's classroom. Not only was her room bright and colourful with displays of the children's work, and buzzing with purposeful activity, but it had an atmosphere of friendliness and co-operation. It didn't take much time in the room to see why. Hardly a minute went by without Ms Patterson commenting in a quiet, positive, and genuine way about someone's work or behaviour: 'I like the way you've done that heading, John. It's really colourful' or 'My goodness you're working hard today, Rachel — well done!' or 'Thanks for picking up that paper on the floor instead of just stepping over it, Mike.'

The children responded to their teacher's praise with a smile, and sometimes a word of appreciation. You could see that it affected their attitude to work in an encouraging and energizing way. No wonder the classroom was a hive of activity. The children also picked up on Ms Patterson's style, and often commented positively on one another's work .

Ms Patterson's philosophy was to focus on success and achievement as much as possible rather than highlighting mistakes and failure. She also made a point of asking her students to assess and evaluate their own work rather than being reliant solely on her judgement:

'So how do you feel about your story, Anna? Are you pleased with it?'

'Yes, I think it's pretty good for me.'

'Which bits do you like best?'

'Well, I like the beginning because it really grabs your attention.'

'Yes, I agree with you. And are there any parts you think could be improved?'

'Maybe I could have used some more dialogue to make the story more interesting.'

'OK. Have another look at it and see what you can do. Let me see what you come up with.'

Ms Patterson's approach encouraged her students during new learning, motivated them to keep trying, and made them aware of their strengths. It helped them to feel competent and confident, while also developing trust in their own judgement.

The same positive approach applies to families. If you think that you've fallen into a rut of negativity with your child, lift yourself out of it through the 'once-a-day' system: find one thing every day, however small it may be, that you can acknowledge, compliment, or appreciate.

Can Praise Be Harmful?

Some writers in the field of child psychology have said that praise is harmful for children because it can lead them to value the praise more than the achievement itself. Because praise is pleasant, children can seek it for its own sake rather than the satisfaction of doing something well, and can become dependent on adult approval. It can also stop them from making up their own minds about the worth of what they do.

Despite the risk of these things happening, for all the reasons discussed in this chapter I think that children do need specific, realistic feedback about their behaviour which highlights what they have done well. It is a very natural human response to express admiration for effort and achievement. The right kind of praise encourages, motivates, and strengthens children, and is an essential aspect of building a healthy self-concept.

In Summary

Praise is food for self-esteem. It encourages children, guides them in their learning, and helps them to become more aware of their personal strengths. To be effective, praise needs to be genuine and specific. Making 'I' statements can help to shape your praise along these lines. Try to include a question to encourage self-evaluation, and remember the 'once-a-day' rule.

11

Low Self-esteem: How to Help

So far, we have looked at the day-to-day things you can do as a parent which will gradually mould and shape your child's self-image in a positive and healthy direction. Children who feel loved, respected, listened to, and secure, are also likely to feel good about themselves. Children who have the opportunity to grow towards independence in an atmosphere where their achievements are recognized and valued are likely to see themselves as competent and worthwhile. Children who belong to a network of social groups, and know their roots, are likely to develop a sense of purpose and worth.

Signs of *high* self-esteem in a young person are:

- A positive, optimistic, energetic approach to life;
- A willingness to try new experiences;
- A sense of trust in their own competence;
- A realistic awareness and acceptance of their strengths and relative weaknesses;
- An ability to evaluate their own performance objectively;
- No strong need for praise from others;
- An ability to accept criticism without defensiveness and hostility;
- An ability to tolerate failure without giving up;
- Valuing and respecting themselves as individuals;
- A feeling that they are in control of their own lives;
- An accepting, friendly, respectful attitude to others; and
- No desire to hurt or feel superior to others.

Indicators of possible *low* self-esteem in a young person are the opposite of the above, in other words:

- A negative, pessimistic, or passive approach to life;
- A reluctance to try new experiences;
- A lack of trust in their own competence;
- A lack of self-awareness;
- An inability to evaluate their strengths and deficits objectively;
- A strong need for reassurance and praise from others;
- An inability to accept criticism without defensiveness or hostility;
- A tendency to overreact to failure;
- A low or negative opinion of themselves;
- A sense of being helpless, powerless, and ineffective;
- A negative, mistrustful, or hostile attitude to others;
- A need to hurt or feel superior to others.

It is easy to diagnose low self-esteem in children who come across as withdrawn, lacking in confidence, and generally rather fearful of life, but a wide range of different symptoms can have the same root cause. For example, children who seem overly confident and boastful may be compensating for serious self-doubt that they cannot admit to or accept in themselves. Youngsters who present as perfectionist, and highly critical of both themselves and others, may be protecting a fragile self-concept.

In adolescents, a persistently hostile attitude may be a defence against the possible uncovering of what they see as an inadequacy or weakness. For the perpetual joker, the laughter of others is reassurance that he is popular and likeable. Risky and self-destructive behaviour, such as promiscuous sex and drug abuse, can be a very dramatic way for a teenager to say, 'I have no respect for myself — I am worthless.'

When Can You Help?

Although children are beginning to be aware of themselves as distinct individuals by the age of two or three, in my experience a true self-concept — an awareness of one's own characteristics together with the ability to evaluate them — does not start to develop until about the age of four or five at the earliest. By six or seven years of age, most children are able to reflect on their own qualities and behaviour in relation to a standard of some sort, and make a judgement about whether they measure up or not. In this way, day by day, experience by experience, their self-esteem starts to take on either a positive or a negative hue. If you think that your child's self-esteem is developing in a negative direction, what can you do about it?

Firstly, that depends on the age of your child. Most of the techniques I discuss in this chapter can only be used with children who are at least seven or eight years old, because they require a certain level of intellectual development to understand and apply them. Below the age of about eight (depending on your child's maturity) you are best to concentrate on doing the simple everyday things we have already discussed which create the basic foundations of healthy self-esteem:

- Make sure they feel loved for the person they are, with no strings attached.
- Express your affection verbally, physically, and often.
- Make time for them, doing things that they like.
- Listen to them and talk with them.
- Ask their opinion.
- Encourage their independence.
- Help them to learn new skills.
- Have confidence in their competence.
- Acknowledge effort and achievement with praise.
- Give freedom of choice within clearly defined limits.

If you are doing most of these things, you can be almost certain that whatever other problems your child may have, poor self-esteem won't be one of them.

Personality

Before we go on to discuss what can be done to help children with low self-esteem, it needs to be mentioned that sometimes an apparent lack of self-confidence in children is not due to their life experiences. Some children just seem to be born more shy and retiring than others. From an early age, despite lots of love, support, and encouragement from their parents, they find it hard to make new friends or to be assertive in social situations. When it comes to new experiences, they tend to hang back rather than dive in.

If you are fairly sure that you are doing most of the things listed in the previous section, which should promote the development of healthy self-esteem, and your child still tends to be a reluctant starter in most social or new learning situations, then you may have to accept that this is simply part of the child's basic personality. If it is, then that tendency to avoid or withdraw from, rather than approach, will probably always be part of their personal style.

This means that as a parent you have a delicate balancing act to perform. On the one hand you must continue to encourage them to take part in new activities, and give them the opportunity to learn new skills, but on the other hand you don't want to place them under the pressure of constantly having to do things that don't come naturally or easily to them.

If your child usually approaches new situations hesitantly and reluctantly, and tries to avoid them, it may mean that she or he may not get the chance to try them out unless you are pushing from behind. The difficult judgement comes in knowing how hard and how far to push before it becomes counter-productive.

Sometimes a bit of nudging will give your child the chance to find out that the new experience they have dreaded is, in fact, a lot of fun, and that they can manage it quite well. Sometimes, however, it becomes clear that no amount of enticement, practice, or prodding will make them enjoy an activity or become any better at it. Time then to flag it away and try something else, learning more about your child's strengths and weaknesses as you go.

Self-talk

When we approach new or challenging situations we bring with us a history of previous experiences which colour our attitude. Previous success in similar tasks or settings will probably make our attitude optimistic, while previous failure may well mean just the opposite. Along with these feelings of confidence or apprehension may go a little verbal commentary to ourselves which we usually aren't even aware of, such as: 'Gulp! I don't like the look of this. The last time I tried it I made a real fool of myself. How can I make an excuse to get out of it?' Or: 'Hey! This looks good! I can handle it, no sweat. Now, how do I get started?'

It is almost certain that we will not be aware of these internal comments, partly because they flash through our mind so quickly, and partly because they may be in the form of images and memories rather than words, but they can certainly have a major effect on our behaviour. In fact, they can become like an audiotape played to ourselves, or a computer program that controls our responses automatically, almost below the level of conscious awareness.

If children lack self-confidence, it may be that the things they say to themselves, the subliminal 'tapes' they play in certain situations, are negative in character rather than positive.

Fortunately, it is possible to record over and erase these tapes by getting children to talk to themselves in a different, more positive way in situations that they find hard to handle. With coaching and encouragement, children can learn to substitute encouraging statements for pessimistic, self-defeating ones. For example:

- 'I can do this.'
- 'I'm going to give this my best shot.'
- 'I'm a bit nervous about this, but so what — just go for it.'
- 'Maybe I'm not the best in the class at this, but at least I can try hard.'
- 'If I don't give it a try, I don't know what I might be able to do.'

If children shrink from getting involved in certain activities, it could be worth giving them a coaching session on positive self-talk.

First of all, listen carefully to how they feel about the problem situation, along the lines discussed in Chapter 5. Try to see the problem through their eyes, and experience it from their perspective. Next, explain to them how we often talk to ourselves about the things we do, and how what we say can either help us or hold us back.

Then, discuss some of the things they could say which would be encouraging rather than discouraging. Work out ways of saying them that feel comfortable and right, preferably making them as short and punchy as possible.

Finally, ask your child to imagine that she or he is actually in the problem situation, making these positive statements. Get them to practise saying them out loud first, as convincingly and enthusiastically as they can, then in a whisper, and finally, in their head.

The new skill then needs to be transferred to real-life settings. Sometimes you will be there on the spot, to prompt, remind, and encourage, but often your coaching will have to be after the event. As with learning any new skill, it will take a while before it supplants old habits, so be prepared to hang in there for the duration.

In my experience, it is not possible to teach these procedures effectively to children younger than about eight years of age, because they simply don't have the abstract thinking skills or self-generated motivation required. Eight- to nine-year-olds should be able to manage them, with quite a lot of ongoing practice and support, and the chances of success will improve with each passing year after that.

If the problem is school-based, you may be able to get your child's teacher to join in the programme with you by prompting and encouraging in the relevant situations, especially at the primary-school level. In the secondary schools it is much more difficult to do this because of the number of teachers involved.

Problem-solving

Positive self-talk is likely to improve your child's motivation to take on tasks which seem difficult, but she or he will probably also need a plan of attack to deal with them successfully. For this, your child will require instruction in the gentle art of problem-solving, which requires a different kind of self-talk.

Problem-solving is another of those skills where, for adults in particular, many of the processes involved take place at a barely conscious level. If we want to teach children how to solve a problem, we have to analyse it as a task, and break it down into a sequence of explicit steps, as follows:

1   What is the Problem?

Step number one is to help your child to be clear about what the problem actually is. This does two things. Firstly, it may help to reduce what seems to be an overwhelming difficulty down to a manageable size. A dreaded situation can seem a little less so when it is taken out of the realm of vague emotions, and pinned down in plain and simple words — a named fear can lose some of its power. If your child is old enough to read and write reasonably fluently, it can help if they write down the problem. There is something about the process of translating a worry into marks on a piece of paper that can make it seem much less daunting — a bit like a scary shape in the dark which turns out to be quite harmless when the light is switched on.

It may also be that your child has magnified the problem, taking one small incident and turning it into a disaster. For example, a quarrel with a friend can become 'Nobody likes me', or a poor mark on a test can be magnified into 'I'll never be any good at maths'. Being specific about the problem can help to combat this.

Secondly, making a problem explicit clarifies what can be done about it. Once the difficulty has been spelt out, it should become much easier to see what the next step might be, and to come up with some possible solutions. For example, there is some chance of dealing with 'The teacher won't answer my questions in maths class' but not much hope of solving 'I hate school!' Sometimes children find it reasonably easy to bring the problem into focus, but usually it requires quite a lot of patience and good listening on your part to help them be specific and concrete about it.

2   How Can I Approach the Problem?

Once the problem has been targeted clearly, sit down together and brainstorm a list of possible solutions. When you do this, be as relaxed and imaginative as you can,

Sit down together and sort out the problem.

ignoring for the minute whether the ideas you come up with are practical or not, for two reasons:

- It allows your creativity greater freedom to operate and to generate fresh ideas; and
- It gives the subtle but important message that problems don't have to be taken seriously, and that treating them in a relaxed and even joking way can make it easier to deal with them. It can also help us to see them more realistically.

So get a big piece of paper and note down any ideas at all that come to mind. Don't censor your thoughts — if you think of it, say it and write it down, no matter how silly it might sound. What seems at first to be a slightly crazy idea might become the germ of a useful plan.

Only after the ideas have dried up do you then start to look at them from the perspective of what would be realistic and workable. Eliminate the way-out ones, which have now served their purpose of freeing up your thinking, and concentrate on a few which show some promise. Weigh up their pros and cons, then settle on one to try.

3   Make a Plan

Next, make a specific, step-by-step plan. Let's say that your child's original, vague statement was: 'Nobody at school likes me.' Patient good listening has helped to sharpen up the picture so that you can see that she is in fact unhappy about being left out of lunchtime games. Brainstorming leads to thinking about options, such as not ever going to school again, taking a board game to play in the library at lunchtimes, learning better social skills, or becoming a black belt in a martial art so that the other kids would be too scared not to include her.

Eliminating the impractical ideas, and talking through the pros and cons for the rest, will narrow the field down to learning better social skills, which means learning how to ask to be included in the games, and how to be a good sport.

Then comes the actual plan of attack, a strategy for turning the goal into reality. This will probably involve some pretend practice in things like how to choose a group where she is likely to be accepted, how to approach the group and ask to play, and ways of behaving which will make other children enjoy her company — for example, sharing, taking turns, and not making fun of others.

Having a plan, talking it through, and practising it with

you may well give your child the confidence to give it a go, rather than give it away, the next time a problem comes up.

4   *How Did It Go?*

After the plan has been put into action in a real-life setting, it will need to be evaluated. Which parts were successful? Which parts weren't? Which parts should be thrown out, and which can be fine-tuned? It's unlikely that everything will go smoothly on the first attempt, so be prepared to provide a troubleshooting-and-support service for a while. Perhaps the most important thing you can do is to reinforce the message that problems can be dealt with if we:

- Are clear about what the problem is;
- Brainstorm as many solutions as we can;
- Choose one that's likely to work;
- Develop a plan;
- Try it;
- Fine-tune it.

Self-talk is also an essential part of the problem-solving process in several different ways. Children need to :

- Remind and prompt themselves to use their plan when they come up against a difficult situation;
- Talk themselves through the steps they have practised;
- Praise themselves for any success they have, saying things like 'Hey! That was good! I did it!' or 'I did really well there, just like I planned!'

Another useful self-talk skill is to make sure that the problem is not being magnified out of proportion. Children can be helped to guard against turning one quarrel into 'Everybody hates me!' or problems with one school subject into 'I'm hopeless at school!' by being encouraged to see the situation objectively at the problem-identification stage.

When we are feeling down and discouraged about a problem, we can punish ourselves needlessly by assuming that it is all our fault, or reading too much into one little incident, or turning a minor failure into a major disaster. To avoid this, teach your child (1) to state the problem as realistically and unemotionally as they can, then (2) to follow it with a 'but', which points out the positive side. For example: 'I had a fight with Joanne, *but* ...

- ... the last time this happened we were friends again the next day.'
- ... it doesn't matter because I'm still friends with Kim.'
- ... she seems a bit grumpy today, so I don't think it's anything I've done.'

The same method can be used in other situations that have the potential to damage self-esteem:

- 'I find it really hard to understand maths, *but* I got good grades in the English and biology tests.'
- 'I guess I'll never be very good at football, *but* I'm one of the better kids in the class at swimming.'
- 'OK, so I am a lot shorter than other kids my age, *but* that doesn't stop me from doing everything just as well as they can.'
- 'Maybe I am overweight, *but* if I exercise a bit more I could do something about that.'
- 'So I'm no movie star to look at, *but* I do have an outgoing personality.'

In summary, the basic principles behind the use of self-talk to boost self-esteem are:

- To be aware of negative self-statements that can undermine self-confidence;
- To replace these negative statements with positive and encouraging statements;

- To use the four-step problem-solving method (including self-praise for success); and
- To look for those positive features and assets that can be buried under a pile of pessimism.

Depending on the age of the child and the amount of practice they have had, all these different kinds of self-talk can be done either in a quiet voice, a whisper, or mentally. The younger the child or the less established the habit, the more likely that the self-talk will have to be done in a quiet voice or whisper. The older the child and the more practice they have had, the more likely it is that they will be able to do it mentally.

I Can

I mentioned in the chapter on school that teachers can help children to focus on their strengths by getting them to keep an 'I can … ' list — in other words, a list of their skills and achievements. Parents, of course, are in a very good position to do just the same, and there's no reason why children can't keep a similar list, or an 'I'm good at … ' list at home. If, for example, your child tends to dwell on their failures and inadequacies, you can help to throw a spotlight on the positive by getting them to write down the things they can do, and do well.

Going through the process of putting strengths and achievements on paper firstly brings them clearly to mind, then, as written words, gives them more reality and substance. Once the list has been started, keep it pinned up for reference at times when self-esteem is sagging, and add to it as new skills are mastered. Alternatively, your child might prefer to keep such a list privately in a desk or diary. Where and how they keep it is not as important as actually having it.

Perfectionism

Some children set such high standards for themselves that they can regard even an above-average performance as a failure — nothing less than excellence is considered good enough. While it is a positive thing for children to strive to achieve their best, if their sense of self-worth depends on coming first or getting an 'A', then their psychological adjustment is clearly at risk. If we need to be the 'top' to feel good about ourselves, it suggests that our self-image is basically shaky and fragile. It means that we have difficulty accepting anything as part of our self-image which is less than perfect, and that is simply unrealistic.

When children evaluate their behaviour and achievements, the 'grade' they give themselves will depend on their standards. Perfectionists set such high standards for themselves that, in their eyes, they fail more often than they succeed. They may feel discouraged and depressed about things they have done, or aspects of themselves, which others would find it hard to fault.

If your child is like this, you first need to ask yourself if you are placing pressure on them, either obvious or subtle, to achieve at high levels or meet high expectations for their behaviour. If you can be fairly sure that you aren't, then talk through the situations that are discouraging your child, looking in particular at how they measure success and failure. The issue may be getting good grades in school tests, their personal appearance, being selected for a sports team, or being included in a certain social group.

Ask questions such as 'What would you be happy with?', 'What would be a successful outcome for you?', 'What sort of result would make you feel OK about yourself?', 'At what point do you switch from "That's acceptable for me" to "That's not acceptable"?', 'What's the bottom line for you to feel good about yourself in regard to this?'

In this way you can help your child begin to think about how they evaluate themselves and their behaviour, and to ask themselves whether their judgements are realistic. If their standards for success and acceptability are unreasonably high, try to help them see that they are setting themselves up for unnecessary, self-inflicted feelings of failure.

Criticism

As children grow towards independence, it is our job as parents to guide, teach, and support them in learning a huge range of tasks in such areas as self-care, appropriate social behaviour, sports and hobbies, getting on with friends, and coping with schoolwork. Part of this job is to point out mistakes, better ways of doing things, and, quite often, to make it clear that certain behaviours are unacceptable. The way we do this can have a significant effect on our children's self-image. Constant fault-finding and criticism are clearly going to make it more difficult for children to develop a sense of confidence and competence, and a feeling that they are OK as people.

Probably most parents are well aware now of the importance of separating the behaviour from the person when you criticize. Try not to say things like 'You're hopeless!' or 'What an idiot!', even though that may be your first thought. It's better if you can focus on the behaviour itself, preferably combined with an 'I' statement. If you say, 'I think that was a silly thing to do' or 'I really don't like it when you speak to me like that', you are much more likely to be able to discuss what happened, and turn it into a learning experience, than if you condemn or abuse the child. Name-calling creates feelings of hurt, anger, and resentment, not a readiness to look at behaviour and how it could be changed.

Another risk with name-calling is that children will sometimes make a point of acting up to the label you give them. Call your child a lazy slob or a cheeky tart, and they may deliberately prove you right as a way of punishing you — 'So you think I'm a slob? OK, I'll show you!'

Think about the standards you hold for your child. If you tend to be ambitious or a perfectionist yourself, with high expectations for their behaviour, criticism may be much more common in your home than praise. Stress and pressure can also force us into a rut of impatience and negativity, so that only shortcomings are noticed and commented on.

You might find it useful to keep a record for a day of the number and kind of comments you make to your child about their behaviour. If fostering self-esteem is your aim, then praise, encouragement, and recognition of effort should well and truly outweigh criticism. If the balance is tipping the other way, think about whether you are expecting too much, or if some other kind of pressure is causing you to pay attention only to things that go wrong. And if that's the case, remember the 'praise once a day' rule.

Helping

Damaged self-esteem can sometimes be repaired by helping others. Doing things for other people often brings with it a good feeling, which has been called 'helper's high'. Part of that feeling is the sense of having achieved something worthwhile, and this can be a healing, strengthening experience for children and young people with a negative self-image.

A good example of this that I have seen involves older primary-school children who are below average in reading. Because reading is such a central part of the school day, below-average readers can feel bad about themselves, especially if they are senior primary-school pupils who have been receiving extra assistance for some years. However, if these children are given the chance to hear and coach young beginning readers — which is often within their range of skills — their usual role is reversed. They become the teacher and helper, and their confidence and self-esteem can receive a major boost as a result.

I have seen the same principle work in an alternative school for disruptive secondary-school students, which runs a community service component as part of their programme. Teenagers who come to the school are often aggressive, unco-operative, and defiant in their regular schools, usually because of a history of academic failure with resulting low self-esteem. But these same students can show patience, kindness, and good humour when working as helpers in a daycare centre, a school for the physically disabled, or a retirement home for the elderly. This is because their assistance in these places is appreciated and valued, so they can start to value themselves more highly, and feel better about themselves as a result. Because the students' contributions are seen as useful and worthwhile, they can start to change their self-image to match.

Unfortunately, it is a bit harder for parents to achieve results like this by giving children the chance to help around the home. For some reason it is usually difficult to get children motivated to do things for mum and dad, or little brother, even with the promise that they will feel a warm glow inside for lending a hand! You will probably have better luck suggesting a visit with some baking to an elderly neighbour, collecting for a good cause, or taking part in a local conservation activity. Despite the old saying, for most children charity seems to begin *outside* the home!

Drama

For children who lack self-confidence, especially in social situations, drama school can provide the opportunity to learn new skills in a safe, enjoyable but challenging environment. A professional drama teacher will lead students through a series of exercises and experiences so that they develop the skills and confidence to perform on stage. But these skills will almost certainly transfer to everyday situations, with obvious benefits for children who find it hard to interact confidently with people.

Drama can give children the chance to:

- Speak out in front of others;
- Take risks;
- Overcome their fear of trying new things;
- Express and deal with strong feelings such as anger, fear, love, and loneliness;
- Enjoy the experience of being centre stage and larger than life;
- Be an indispensable part of a team effort when productions are staged.

Through the use of role play, and the empowering effect of imagination, children can practise dealing with situations they find difficult to cope with in everyday life. Pretending to be brave, outgoing, assertive, or decisive on stage can carry over to school and home.

If you think your child could benefit from taking part in drama classes, ask at their school or check the local paper for available courses. Before signing on, however, discuss your child's needs with the teacher to make sure that the course offers the kinds of experience that could be helpful for them.

Counselling

The suggestions in this chapter should be helpful if the balance of your child's self-esteem tends to tip towards the negative, but if she or he seems to have many of the signs of low self-esteem that were discussed at the beginning of this chapter, or has some of them to a marked degree, then you might need to seek professional help. For example, if she or he:

- seems to have a very negative self-image,
- usually approaches most new experiences reluctantly or fearfully,
- is very sensitive to failure or criticism,
- often uses words like 'dumb', 'useless', or 'stupid' to describe herself or himself,
- is often tearful or depressed,

then you probably need some professional guidance and support. Most children will show some of these signs occasionally, or perhaps in particular settings, but if these become their usual responses to most situations, then it's unlikely you will be able to help them through it on your own.

One important reason for this is that as a parent you are emotionally involved in your child's behaviour, so it is hard to remain calm, objective, and patient about it. It is just too easy to become frustrated, over-anxious, or angry — emotions which will make things worse rather than better.

A professional counsellor, on the other hand, can remain emotionally detached from the problem, and assess it more realistically, as well as bring a range of helping skills to the situation. Also, however much you may regret it, it is a fact that children are more likely to listen to and accept advice from an outsider than from their own parents.

Another reason why professional help can be valuable is that your child's distress may be related to wider family issues which you cannot see because you are too close to them, or which you may in fact be contributing to in some way without being aware of it. That is why many counsellors prefer to work with the whole family rather than just the individual who seems to have the problem.

Most major centres have counselling agencies which specialize in working with troubled children and their families. Your local public hospital is likely to have a family counselling service; government education departments often have a psychological service; and most secondary schools have a guidance counsellor. In addition, there will be private agencies as well as individual psychologists and counsellors listed in the telephone book. If you are not sure about whom to approach, your family doctor or school principal should be able to suggest someone.

Before you make an appointment, ask about the background of the person you will be seeing, making sure that they are qualified and experienced in working with children. Because different therapists use different methods in working with families, you are also entitled to know the approach they will take. Don't be embarrassed to ask about this, about the probable length of treatment, and also about fees.

In Summary

In this chapter we have looked at the signs of high and low self-esteem, and some techniques which parents can use to help children whose self-concept is sagging. The most important of these techniques are positive self-talk and the skills of problem-solving, because they can be applied to so many different situations.

Activities that are also potentially useful for children with low self-esteem are keeping an 'I can' list, taking on the role of helper, and attending a drama class. Be aware of the harmful effects of criticism and how perfectionism can sabotage self-esteem. Finally, seek professional help if your child shows signs of serious damage to their sense of self-worth.

12

In Conclusion

Self-esteem is a fundamental factor affecting how we cope with life. It has a decisive influence on our ability to function as effective, independent, emotionally stable individuals. Our approach to life can vary from confident, positive, and optimistic, to hesitant, negative, and pessimistic, depending on our sense of self-worth. And, as we know, our approach and outlook have a major effect on what we actually achieve.

Self-esteem is shaped during childhood. Because of its power, one of our more important tasks as parents is to send our children out into the world with as strong and healthy a self-concept as we can nurture. Helping you to do that has been the purpose of this book. In these pages I have tried to address what I see as the major factors in promoting the development of self-esteem. Let's briefly go over those again.

I have no doubt that unconditional love comes first in the list. Without the feeling that they are loved and valued by their parents, children will have no solid foundation on which to build a stable and secure sense of self-worth. We express this love through physical affection, words, and making sure that our children's basic needs are met, not just their basic biological needs, but also their needs for encouragement towards independence, and for respect.

We demonstrate respect for our children through recognition of their rights and uniqueness as individuals, and awareness that they are our responsibility, not our property. We also show respect by making the effort to really listen to them and, as they get older, by giving them the opportunity to make choices and trusting them to do the right thing.

It is also important to be aware of and respect the pattern of strengths and abilities which makes each child a unique person, doing what we can to foster development without forcing it, and without being blinkered by gender stereotypes.

A democratic parenting style benefits self-esteem by giving children the opportunity to discuss issues that affect their daily lives, to exercise judgement, and to make choices within limits. Encouraging children to do these things promotes the development of their independence, responsibility, assertiveness, and self-confidence.

Belonging to groups of different kinds can give children a sense of identity and of their place in the world. It also gives them the chance to learn new skills, and experience feelings of accomplishment, pride, and of being a valued team member.

Finally, regular doses of praise nourish the growth of self-esteem. The right kind of praise guides and encourages children in their learning, recognizes their efforts and achievements, and affirms their strengths.

Children who grow up in a home environment where most of these things are valued and practised are likely to:

- Have a strong and stable sense of self-worth;
- Be independent, confident, optimistic, and assertive;
- Value and respect themselves as individuals;
- Perceive their strengths and relative weaknesses realistically;
- Trust in their own ability;
- Accept failure or criticism without giving in or becoming defensive; and
- Be friendly to and accepting of others, without the need to put them down or hurt them.

While I am highlighting the positive characteristics of children with high self-esteem, it would, of course, be unrealistic to think that they behaved positively all the time, or to imagine them as a species of saintly superkids. While they may show these desirable behaviours more often than most children, they will also be as silly, sassy, and selfish as any child can be from time to time. And there will certainly be some situations where they are hesitant, anxious, or self-critical.

The point is that children with high self-esteem have a stable, positive core to their personality which helps them to ride out the challenges and setbacks of life with a better-than-even chance of success. But that doesn't mean that they won't occasionally drive you nuts!

It would also be a mistake to think that to nurture high self-esteem in children you have to dotingly make them the sole focus and centre of your life. That would be counter-productive, and more likely to produce a child who is demanding, dissatisfied, and dependent. Children are important, but cannot always have first call on your time, attention, and energy.

I am sure that you are already doing much of what I have suggested in this book. Some of the ideas in it will be new to you, and you will want to try them out. Others you will want to think about a little, and others you may perhaps disagree with. In any case, I hope you will talk about them with your partner or a friend. And, at the very least, I hope that reading this book will in some way strengthen and enrich your relationship with your child.